INTERNATIONAL DEVELOPMENT IN PRACTICE

Developing Entrepreneurial Ecosystems for Digital Businesses and Beyond

A Diagnostic Toolkit

MARCIO CRUZ AND TINGTING JUNI ZHU

WORLD BANK GROUP

Contents

Boxes

Figures

Maps

Tables

Online Appendixes

Online appendixes A through F are available at https://openknowledge.worldbank.org /handle/10986/40305.

Acknowledgments

This report was prepared as part of the World Bank analytical and advisory service tasks "Entrepreneurship and New Digital Businesses Models" (P167399) and "Digital Entrepreneurial Ecosystem Diagnostics" (P169557) under the Trade, Investment, and Competitiveness Global Unit, as part of the Finance, Competitiveness, and Innovation Global Practice. A World Bank team led by Marcio Cruz and Tingting Juni Zhu prepared the toolkit under the overall supervision and guidance of Mona Haddad, Martha Martinez Licetti, and Denis Medvedev. David B. Audretsch (Indiana University) provided overall guidance as senior adviser. The peer reviewers at the World Bank were Zenaida Hernandez Uriz, Natasha Kapil, Smita Kuriakose, and Gaurav Nayyar. The core team included Besart Avdiu, Prasanna Lal Das, Philip Grinsted, Justin Hill, Ryan Chia Kuo, Santiago Reyes Ortega, Jesica Torres Coronado, Malathi Velamuri, and Douglas Zhihua Zeng. The team is grateful for valuable feedback and comments from the external reviewers: Inge Graef (Tilburg University), Gary Ross (partner, Ross Law Group, PLLC), and Erik Stam (Utrecht University). Other World Bank staff, including Xavier Cirera, Ami Dalal, Fatou Fadika, Mary C. Hallward-Driemeier, Ernesto Lopez-Córdova, Bill Maloney, and Hangyul Song, also provided key input and feedback.

This report resulted from pilots in several countries. Laurent Corthay, Marcio Cruz, Mark Dutz, Carlos Rodríguez-Castelán, Meriem Slimane, Jesica Torres Coronado, and Trang Tran provided key contributions with regard to Senegal. Pinyi Chen, Marcio Cruz, Jeffrey Dickinson, Subika Farazi, Zenaida Hernandez Uriz, Justin Hill, Leah Kiwara, Lynette Ndile, Cecilia Paradi-Guilford, Maria Perez de Paz, and Jesica Torres Coronado provided key contributions with regard to Kenya. Asya Akhlaque, Philip Grinsted, Nguyen Ha, Sara Nyman, and Tingting Juni Zhu provided key contributions with regard to Vietnam. Lefteris J. Anastasopoulos, Daniel Sokol, Ana Cristina Soria, Tingting Juni Zhu, and Siegfried Zottel provided key contributions with regard to Nigeria. Ana Paula Cusolito, Toni Eliasz, Philip Grinsted, Wycliff Moeletsi Tlhalefang, Justine White, and Tingting Juni Zhu provided key contributions with regard to South Africa. Can Arslan, Pablo Astudillo, Marcio Cruz, Christopher Haley, Natasha Kapil, and Zoe Lu provided key contributions with regard to Romania. Pedro Amo, Marcio Cruz, Mayra de Moran, Gabriela Montenegro, and Jesica Torres Coronado provided key contributions with regard to Central America. Martha Caniceros, Esperanza Lasagabaster, Ernesto Lopez-Córdova, Horman Millán, Eduardo Piedra, and Jesica Torres Coronado provided key contributions with regard to Mexico. Aarre Laakso contributed as editor of this toolkit as well as for the pilots in Romania and Central America.

The team also wishes to thank the Competitiveness for Jobs & Economic Transformation (C-JET) Trust Fund and the infoDev Trust Fund for providing the financial support that made this report possible.

About the Authors

Marcio Cruz is a principal economist with the Economic Policy Research unit of the International Finance Corporation. Previously, he was a senior economist with the Finance, Competitiveness, and Innovation Global Practice of the World Bank. His research has focused on firm dynamics, technology adoption, entrepreneurship, international trade, and impact evaluation. He also worked in the Development Economics Vice Presidency, contributing to the World Bank's flagship publications *Global Economic Prospects* and *Global Monitoring Report*. Before joining the World Bank, Cruz was a tenured professor in the Department of Economics at the Federal University of Paraná in Brazil and an economist for the Secretary of Planning of the state of Paraná. His research has been published in scholarly journals such as the *Journal of International Economics*, *Small Business Economics,* and *World Development*. He holds a PhD in international economics from the Graduate Institute in Geneva.

Tingting Juni Zhu is a senior economist at the World Bank based in Washington, DC. She serves as a technical lead in digital business ecosystem and innovation-driven growth topics. Her recent practice covers new knowledge on the industrial organization of platform-based and data-driven businesses. Zhu's scope of work is global, and she has field experience in implementing investment projects and digital market reforms in Africa, the Middle East, Central Asia, and Southeast Asia. Her publications in peer-reviewed journals are in the areas of digital market development and economic geography. She holds graduate degrees from Johns Hopkins University and the Chinese University of Hong Kong.

Abbreviations

COVID-19	coronavirus 2019
DPF	Development Policy Financing
ESO	entrepreneurship support organization
EU	European Union
FCCPA	Federal Competition and Consumer Protection Act (Nigeria)
FCCPC	Federal Competition and Consumer Protection Commission (Nigeria)
FCI	Finance, Competitiveness, and Innovation Global Practice (World Bank)
FY	fiscal year
GEM	Global Entrepreneurship Monitor
GERN	Global Entrepreneurship Research Network
IFC	International Finance Corporation
IO	intermediary organization
IPF	Investment Project Financing
M&E	monitoring and evaluation
MSMEs	micro, small, and medium enterprises
ODR	online dispute resolution
OECD	Organisation for Economic Co-operation and Development
R&D	research and development
SAFE	simple agreement for future equity
SAR	special administrative region
SMEs	small and medium enterprises
SME&E	small and medium enterprises and entrepreneurship
UN	United Nations
UNESCO	United Nations Educational, Scientific, and Cultural Organization
VC	venture capital
WB	World Bank

Introduction to the Toolkit

BACKGROUND

The World Bank has a large portfolio of investments supporting entrepreneurship. These investments are spread across countries in different regions, with varying income levels, and in various World Bank units across the International Bank for Reconstruction and Development, the International Development Agency, and the International Finance Corporation. To support these operations, it is essential to have a solid diagnostic approach that can be adjusted to each country's context and that follows a standard conceptual framework and methodology for identifying key policy priorities to support entrepreneurial ecosystems.

When conducting a diagnostic to identify opportunities to enhance entrepreneurial ecosystems, methodology consistency and use of the best data available are key. Entrepreneurial ecosystem assessments and rankings abound, but they are rarely based on solid economic theory or informed by micro data representative of a country's (or region's) population of firms, particularly in developing countries. These shortcomings are especially relevant when assessing digital entrepreneurial ecosystems and technology-intensive start-ups in the face of increasing country demand for diagnostics and for identifying policy priorities to inform policy makers and practitioners. This demand expanded further during and after the COVID-19 (coronavirus) pandemic, particularly in developing countries.

Staff at the World Bank have designed and piloted a new approach to ecosystem assessments in collaboration with leading academics and practitioners. The new approach builds on previous expertise in collecting and analyzing firm-level data, assessing the quality and efficiency of policies supporting innovation and small and medium enterprise (SME) development, and using insights from spatial economics to support subnational analysis. Rather than building a composite index for cross-country comparisons, this new generation of ecosystem diagnostics provides guidance for observing supply and demand factors and barriers to the efficient allocation of resources within the ecosystem and explicitly considers the quality of entrepreneurship enablers such as incubators and accelerators. The diagnostic tools also provide new methods for identifying potential local or subnational ecosystems in developing countries;

new survey instruments with which to collect data from public programs, enabling organizations, and start-ups; and new data sets to be adapted to the context of developing countries.

This toolkit has specific modules on digital entrepreneurship. Digital entrepreneurs create digital products or services that the wider economy demands. Digital entrepreneurs tend to be different from traditional entrepreneurs because of the characteristics of the underlying digital technologies and associated business models. Digital start-ups tend to be growth-oriented, asset-lite, and knowledge-intensive, with core products built on intangible assets (such as data and intellectual property). For digital entrepreneurship assessments, this toolkit takes advantage of the latest pilot efforts in using new datasets and surveys assembled by the World Bank team. It also summarizes early lessons learned regarding new types of digital market regulations and financing models that would particularly affect digital entrepreneurs.

This toolkit provides practical resources for conducting entrepreneurial ecosystem assessments. It includes a framework, guidelines, and useful tools for performing diagnostics to underpin policies supporting entrepreneurial ecosystems. The conceptual framework helps analysts, practitioners, and policy makers organize the flow of relevant information when assessing how policy can best ignite entrepreneurial forces to harness the potential for economic performance. The toolkit proposes a method for assessing entrepreneurial ecosystems in three stages: (1) context analysis (cross-country benchmarking and local entrepreneurial ecosystems); (2) mapping of public programs, regulations, and intermediary organizations supporting entrepreneurship; and (3) policy options for enhancing ecosystems.

Practitioners can use the output of the diagnostic for several purposes. Across the World Bank, it could be a stand-alone product, such as a report focusing on an entrepreneurial ecosystem, or it could contribute to existing World Bank products. For example, the diagnostic output could form a thematic part of Country Economic Updates, a chapter within a Country Economic Memorandum, or a portion of a Country Private Sector Diagnostic. Diagnostics of digital entrepreneurship can be conducted independently and contribute to Digital Economy Country Diagnostics or other digital transformation–themed products. The analysis can also be conducted by countries, government agencies, or development agencies that need a diagnostic assessment to build a strategic working plan to support entrepreneurship, including digital entrepreneurship. As a result of this diagnostic, practitioners should be able to use data-driven evidence to identify key policy priorities and actionable strategies to bolster policies aiming to boost entrepreneurial activities by increasing the number and quality of impactful businesses (as measured by both high productivity and job creation).

This toolkit summarizes lessons gained from implementing entrepreneurial ecosystem diagnostics to support policies in several countries. The conceptual framework and methodology proposed in this toolkit (Audretsch, Cruz, and Torres 2022) have been piloted for different sectors and countries at different income levels, including Central America—Costa Rica, El Salvador, Guatemala, and Honduras (De Morán et al. 2021), Kenya (Cruz and Hernandez Uriz 2022), Mexico (Lasagabaster et al. 2023), Nigeria (Zottel et al. 2021), Romania (Cruz et al. 2022), Senegal (Cruz, Dutz, and Rodríguez-Castelán 2022), South Africa (White et al. 2022), and Vietnam (Akhlaque et al. 2022). The analyses across these countries focused on different issues, ranging from digital entrepreneurship (see Zhu et al. 2022), to general entrepreneurship performance. These pilots used a methodology that the World Bank team initially designed and subsequently revised based on lessons learned and knowledge accumulated during the pilots between 2019 and 2021. For further details on the pilots, please consult the references cited.

CONTENTS

The toolkit consists of six modules in three parts. The following paragraphs describe the modules in more detail.

Part 1: Context

- *Module 1: Cross-country context analysis.* This module guides readers through generating a snapshot of a country's entrepreneurial ecosystem at the national and subnational levels based on the conceptual framework.

- *Module 2: Assessing local entrepreneurial ecosystems.* This module describes a method for identifying potential local entrepreneurial ecosystems based on economies of agglomeration and by considering the diversity and quality of firms. Practitioners can use this method to select strategic localities for deep-dive analyses and can apply it in the context of developing countries using firm or establishment census data.

- *Module 3: Digital entrepreneurship and tech start-ups.* This module describes how to assess digital entrepreneurship and tech start-ups using a new World Bank longitudinal data set of 200,000 digital businesses in 190 countries. It also describes the specifics to consider when conducting a diagnostic focusing on platform-based or data-driven business models that exert network effects.

Part 2: Mapping

- *Module 4: Mapping public programs and intermediary organizations.* This module describes how to map and analyze a policy mix by identifying and analyzing the characteristics of public programs and intermediary organizations that support entrepreneurship. Practitioners can also tailor this module to include innovation programs in a few local clusters with many digital and knowledge-intensive start-ups. A critical insight from this analysis is the potential for identifying gaps or overlaps of initiatives already in place to prioritize resources for the programs likely to have the greatest impact.

- *Module 5: Digital market regulations.* This module compiles a set of regulations (such as platform regulations and data regulations) that apply to firms adopting digital business models. It covers 13 regulatory topics in a standard survey and has both de jure and de facto questions. After the diagnostics, certain regulatory reforms and enforcement capacity-building programs can be proposed. These regulations would particularly affect firms with digital business models.

Part 3: Policy

- *Module 6: Policy options to support entrepreneurial ecosystems.* This module summarizes how to use the diagnostic conducted through previous modules to identify key gaps and priorities for policy interventions. It provides a list of policy instruments, including references to evidence when available. It also discusses specifics on financing options targeting tech firms that are high-risk–high-return, that are asset-lite, that need to scale quickly, and that require (quasi-)equity risk financing. Finally, it summarizes some of the instruments the World Bank has used to support entrepreneurship programs.

Although each module can be implemented independently and through different stages, there are important complementarities between them. Figure I.1 summarizes how the different modules can be combined when preparing a diagnostic. Modules 1, 2, 4, and 6 can be used to assess entrepreneurial ecosystems in general. If the objective is to focus on digital businesses, the methodology can be adjusted, with greater reliance on modules 3, 4, 5, and 6. Insights for country context and local ecosystems, from modules 1 and 2, can also be adjusted and applied to digital businesses.

The overall guidance in this toolkit will help analysts benefit from the best and most comprehensive data available in the country with which to conduct this exercise. Rather than proposing specific indexes for comparing countries or local ecosystems, this toolkit offers a method that can be used to systematically obtain and analyze firm-level data, which is particularly relevant for developing and emerging economies for which firm-level and administrative data constraints are more prevalent.

FIGURE I.1

How to use different modules for entrepreneurial ecosystem assessments (general and digital)

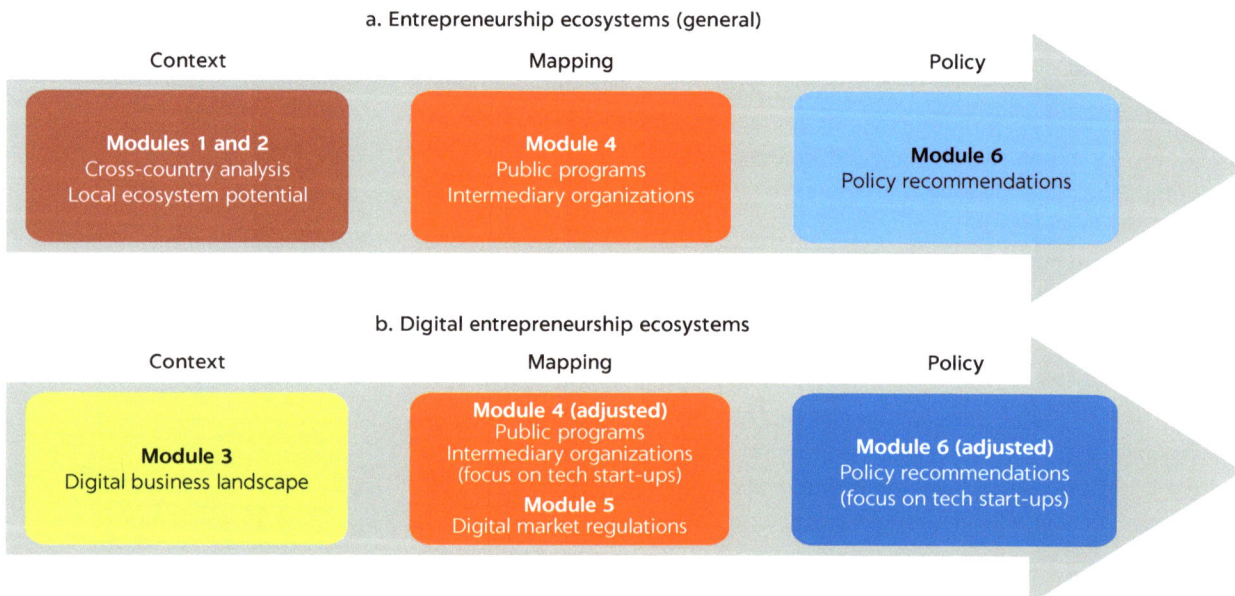

Source: Original figure for this publication.

CONCEPTUAL FRAMEWORK

Understanding entrepreneurial ecosystems

There is no single widely agreed-upon definition of *entrepreneurial ecosystem*.[1] The term *business ecosystem* was introduced by Moore (1993), and multiple definitions continue to be used in various contexts. As a metaphor, the term *ecosystem* echoes the meaning of the word in the natural sciences.[2] In the economic context, the actors include entrepreneurs, workers, investors, researchers, and supporting organizations that provide the resources and constraints to convert ideas and opportunities into businesses.

Starting a business that expands and innovates requires a combination of complementary factors beyond entrepreneurial talent. However, most of those factors, including ideas, human and physical capital, knowledge, and financial instruments, face mobility costs (across both sectors and regions). These costs lead to persistent heterogeneity, both across and within countries, in the availability of resources, and barriers to accessing them surround entrepreneurs and firms. Still, the question remains: how can policy best ignite entrepreneurial forces to harness the potential for economic performance?

In the quest for an answer, thought leaders in research and policy have turned to the strategy of entrepreneurial ecosystems with the explicit goal of igniting entrepreneurship. An entrepreneurial ecosystem characterizes the spatial organization, structure, configuration, and interactions of organizations, firms, institutions, and individuals at a specific geographic place that is conducive to entrepreneurship (Audretsch, Cruz, and Torres 2022). The role of policy is to influence and shape the entrepreneurial ecosystem in such a manner that it generates the desired degree of entrepreneurship. However, because there are many relevant factors interacting in this process, clarity is often lacking on which factors matter most and how to use analytical tools to establish policy priorities for developing or enhancing this environment and making it more conducive to entrepreneurship activity. This problem is particularly relevant in the context of developing countries, where data with which to conduct such diagnostics are not widely available.

This section provides a conceptual framework guiding the methodology proposed in this toolkit for conducting an entrepreneurial ecosystem diagnostic to inform policy recommendations. The conceptual framework is based on Audretsch, Cruz, and Torres (2022), a background paper developed for this report, and a wide review of the literature. It provides the parameters related to entrepreneurship output and the factors that are relevant for the entrepreneur's decision to start a business that has the potential to scale up and innovate. The methodology for implementing the diagnostic is split across three stages (context at the country and subnational levels, mapping of enablers, and policy recommendations), thus taking into consideration the elements described in the conceptual framework and the interaction among them. The implementation of each stage is described in specific modules.

The diagnostic includes specific modules that focus on digital entrepreneurship and tech start-ups. Often, the reference to entrepreneurial ecosystems, both in the literature and among practitioners, focuses on digital and tech start-ups— either firms that are digital providers or that intensively rely on new digital business models (for example, platform-based and data-intensive ones) with the aim of scaling up through innovative products and services. Although the conceptual framework and the methodology proposed in this toolkit can be used in any context or sector or by any type of entrepreneur, two modules (3 and 5) focus on the specifics associated with digital entrepreneurship.

Creating a conceptual framework for entrepreneurial ecosystems

Entrepreneurship plays a critical role in boosting economic growth and creating more and better jobs. In many country contexts, job creation tends to be concentrated among a small share of young firms that grow rapidly in relatively brief spurts. These high-impact businesses operate in many sectors of economic activity and tend to be more innovative, more connected to global value chains, and more likely to benefit from economies of agglomeration. Even if such high-potential start-ups are difficult to identify ahead of time, they are more likely to arise in dynamic ecosystems characterized by complementary factors providing the conditions for (1) high entry rates of (better quality) firms, (2) the capacity of those firms to scale up, and (3) the likelihood that they will promote innovation and technological upgrading.

To contextualize the key functions and output of an entrepreneurial ecosystem, figure I.2 summarizes the entrepreneur's problem to start and scale up a business. First, a potential entrepreneur with a given entrepreneurial talent and managerial skills needs to decide between starting a business or being a wage worker. The entrepreneur combines resources with those available in the ecosystem (for example, ideas, knowledge, physical capital, human capital, other intermediate inputs) to produce goods and services for the market, which will involve interactions with workers, other entrepreneurs, and other firms. To use the resources available in the ecosystem, the entrepreneur will need to have access to finance and play according to the formal (regulatory) and informal

FIGURE I.2

The entrepreneur's problem

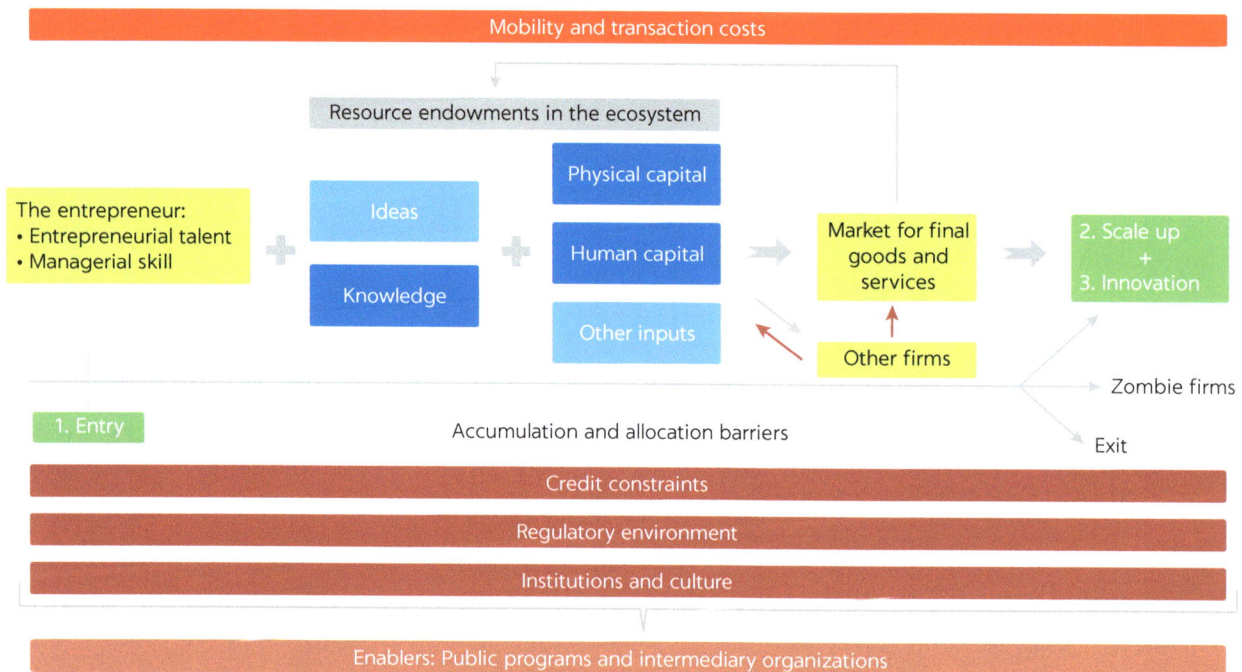

Source: Audretsch, Cruz, and Torres 2022.

(cultural) rules of the game (institutions). The entrepreneur will reach the market for its final goods and services, while interacting with other firms, by competing in similar markets as well as by demanding or providing intermediate goods and services. As a result, it will enter the market as a new business and may succeed (for example, by scaling up and innovating), stay stagnant over time (zombie firms), or exit the market. The geographic space plays a key role in the entrepreneurial ecosystem, given the relevance of mobility and transaction costs for some of those factors (for example, ideas, knowledge, human capital), which results in further interactions at the local level (Audretsch, Cruz, and Torres 2022).

The functions described in the entrepreneur's problem provide the fundamentals of a simplified framework for assessing entrepreneurial ecosystems (figure I.3). First, the framework identifies the key outputs associated with entrepreneurship at the extensive (entry) and intensive (scale up and innovation) margins. These different dimensions capture not only the quantity but also the quality of entrepreneurship, which is critical to analyzing the impact of an entrepreneurial ecosystem. Importantly, in a dynamic perspective they can affect the ecosystem over time (for example, an increasing number of successful entrepreneurs would likely lead to an improvement in the resource endowment). Second, the entrepreneurial ecosystem pillars are defined as key relevant functions that affect the entrepreneur's problem. This toolkit groups these elements into three categories: (1) resource endowments (physical capital, human capital, and knowledge); (2) demand for resources in the ecosystem driven by new entrepreneurs, incumbent firms, and markets; and (3) accumulation and allocation barriers (access to finance, regulations, culture). Audretsch, Cruz,

FIGURE I.3

Entrepreneurial ecosystem: Conceptual framework

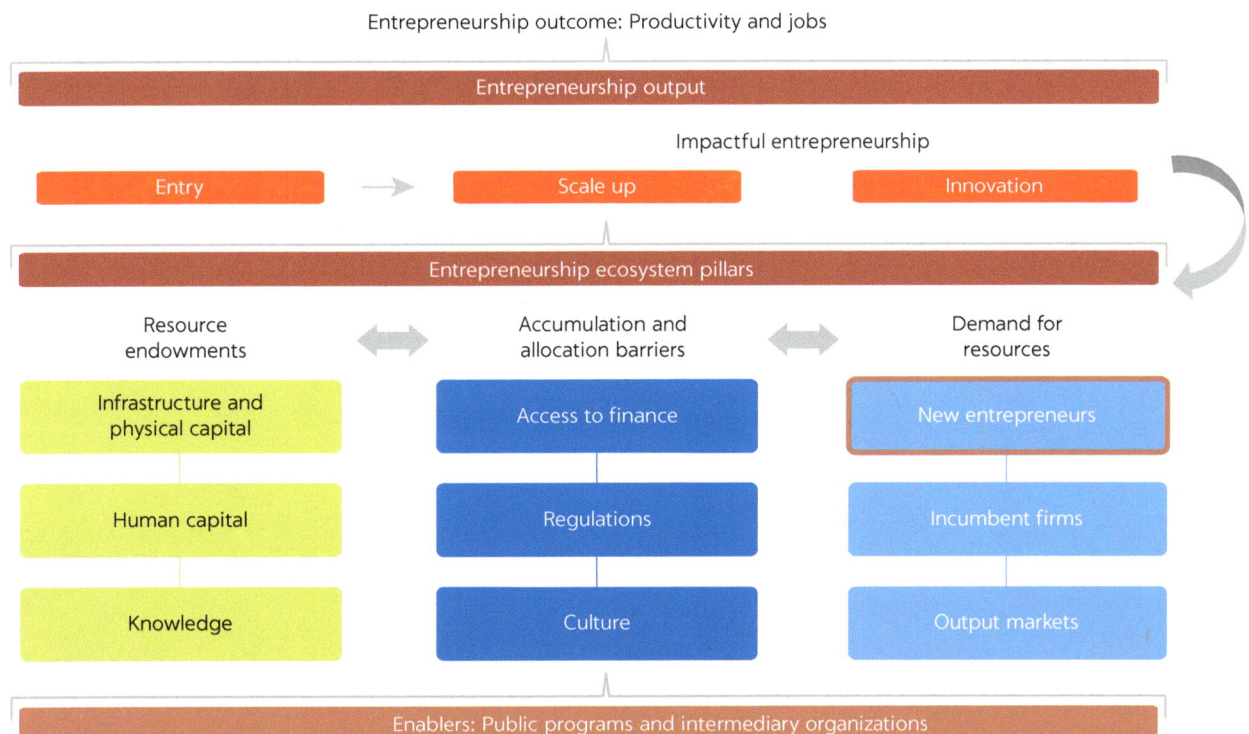

Source: Audretsch, Cruz, and Torres 2022.

and Torres (2022) use an occupational choice model with knowledge-based hierarchies to describe the entrepreneur's problem. In this framework, workers can choose their occupation (for example, work for a wage or be an entrepreneur). If they become an entrepreneur, the framework focuses on their demand toward resources in the ecosystem, including human capital.

Policy makers can influence the entrepreneurial ecosystem to maximize economic growth, and subsequent high-quality job creation, by addressing market failures. In most countries, the essential elements of institutions, networks, and actors that enable entrepreneurship and innovation are missing, underdeveloped, or malfunctioning. Market failures may arise in any of the factors of the entrepreneurial ecosystem. These failures can be associated with the supply, demand, or allocation pillars.[3] Governments can influence an ecosystem directly through policy instruments and regulations or indirectly through ecosystem enablers that support entrepreneurship (bottom of figure I.3).

This conceptual framework builds on a rich literature analyzing entrepreneurial and innovation ecosystems. A large and robust literature identifies and characterizes what constitutes an entrepreneurial ecosystem, along with commensurate policy guidelines (see Acs, Autio, and Szerb 2014; Acs et al. 2017; Andrews et al. 2022; Audretsch and Belitski 2021; Audretsch, Belitski, and Cherkas 2021; Audretsch et al. 2019; Autio and Levie 2017; Cao and Shi 2021; Guzman and Stern 2020; Isenberg 2016; O'Connor and Audretsch 2022; Stam 2015; Szerb et al. 2019; Wurth, Stam, and Spigel 2021). The framework provided in this toolkit is inspired by this literature as well as by the national innovation system framework developed by Maloney (2017). This framework is also aligned with the approaches proposed by Leendertse, Schrijvers, and Stam (2021) and Stam and Van de Ven (2021) through its emphasis on the inputs and outputs of entrepreneurship activities.

The importance of the local environment

Many of these complementary factors face mobility costs across sectors and regions, meaning that the local environment surrounding the firm is critical to enhancing productivity and competitiveness and providing resources to entrepreneurs.[4] Even businesses that significantly rely on connections through global value chains still depend on access to resources that are used locally.

A vigorous and dynamic entrepreneurial ecosystem is critical, but it requires investment and time to mature. For this reason, identifying the potential of entrepreneurial ecosystems at the sector-regional level provides the opportunity to target interventions to areas with more potential. Evidence suggests that improving management and technological capabilities, facilitating access to markets and finance, and providing more information and knowledge can be effective in improving business outcomes. Many of the interventions that are needed to address these challenges face barriers to scaling up. By identifying local high-potential entrepreneurial ecosystems, policy makers can target experiments and interventions to an environment that provides greater possibilities of spillover effects, which is critical to scaling up.[5]

Entrepreneurial ecosystem assessment

This toolkit proposes a methodology for assessing entrepreneurial ecosystems in three stages: (1) context analysis, (2) mapping of enablers, and (3) policy recommendations. If a country would like to focus on tech or digital entrepreneurs, it can conduct the digital entrepreneurship assessment independently, following the same three stages of analysis. The conceptual framework remains the same, but certain supply and demand factors, along with digital market policies, would be more relevant to digital entrepreneurs.

The first stage (context analysis) provides a snapshot of the country's entrepreneurial ecosystem at the national and subnational levels, based on the conceptual framework (figure I.4). The snapshot focuses on ecosystem-level entrepreneurship performance output and outcome indicators. These analyses are complemented by an in-depth discussion of the ecosystem pillars (or initial conditions) of supply factors, demand factors, and barriers to accumulation and allocation. This context analysis has been explored by other entrepreneurial ecosystem assessment methodologies. The main added value from the proposed methodology is that it (1) incorporates more firm-level and administrative data to assess entrepreneurship outcomes for developing countries,[6] (2) expands the use of experimental tools to gather more up-to-date entrepreneurship indicators at lower cost, (3) generates more comparable entrepreneurship indicators at the subnational level, and (4) provides instruments to assess the policy mix.

The second stage provides an assessment of the policy mix and identifies the gaps in policy instruments and institutional capabilities. Typically, countries have several policy instruments that support entrepreneurship, but without an overall picture of their main objectives and budget allocation. This lack of information leads to a higher probability of overlap and a lack of consistency between policies and the development goals of the ecosystem. In many developing countries, particularly low-income countries, this issue also extends to programs supported by donors. The same applies to intermediary organizations (public or private). This toolkit seeks to collect and analyze data at the policy instrument

FIGURE I.4

Entrepreneurial ecosystem assessment: Stages of analysis

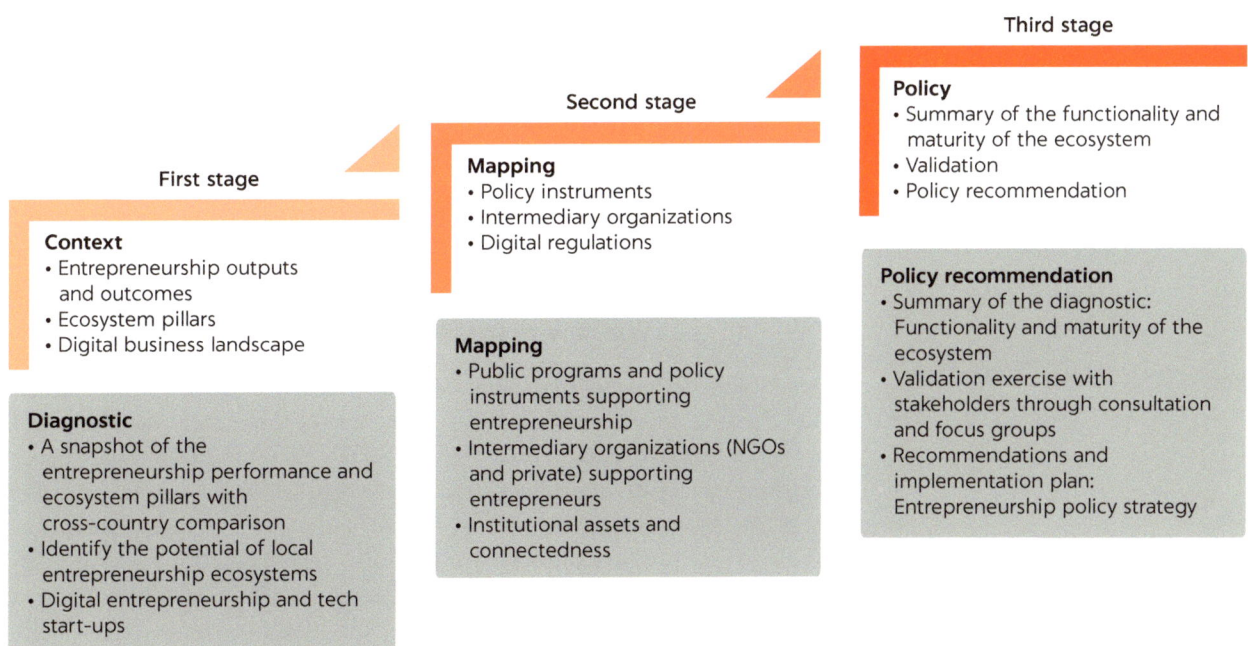

Third stage

Policy
- Summary of the functionality and maturity of the ecosystem
- Validation
- Policy recommendation

Second stage

Mapping
- Policy instruments
- Intermediary organizations
- Digital regulations

First stage

Context
- Entrepreneurship outputs and outcomes
- Ecosystem pillars
- Digital business landscape

Diagnostic
- A snapshot of the entrepreneurship performance and ecosystem pillars with cross-country comparison
- Identify the potential of local entrepreneurship ecosystems
- Digital entrepreneurship and tech start-ups

Mapping
- Public programs and policy instruments supporting entrepreneurship
- Intermediary organizations (NGOs and private) supporting entrepreneurs
- Institutional assets and connectedness

Policy recommendation
- Summary of the diagnostic: Functionality and maturity of the ecosystem
- Validation exercise with stakeholders through consultation and focus groups
- Recommendations and implementation plan: Entrepreneurship policy strategy

Source: Original figure for this publication.

Note: NGOs = nongovernmental organizations.

and institution levels. This analysis builds on the World Bank's expertise on conducting public expenditure review focused on science, technology, and innovation (Cirera and Maloney 2017; Correa 2014). It also identifies connections between ecosystem actors through network visualization to identify gaps and underserved areas in the ecosystem.

The third stage refers to the identification of key policy priorities validated by stakeholders and proposes policy recommendations. The diagnostic combining the cross-country analysis, the characterization of the potential of the local ecosystem, and the mapping of enablers should be used to define policy priorities. As part of this process, it is important not only to consult stakeholders (actors) to obtain relevant information on the quality of the functions, interactions, and impact of the entrepreneurial ecosystem but also to validate the key priorities and policy recommendations resulting from the assessment. In this stage, focus group interviews with entrepreneurs, intermediary organizations, and policy makers are implemented to identify the key gaps in governance, interaction between stakeholders, and policy design and implementation. The three-stage entrepreneurial ecosystem assessment leads to a final report with a Plan of Recommendations and Implementation.

The proposed approach described in this toolkit complements several other initiatives aiming to assess entrepreneurial ecosystems. Table I.1 summarizes some standard instruments available, including the Global Entrepreneurship Monitor, the Startup Genome, the Global Entrepreneurship Index, and the OECD SME and Entrepreneurship Outlook. Most of these instruments aim to provide standard indicators that are comparable across countries or local ecosystems. These instruments rarely combine a comprehensive approach with a country-level context, use representative firm-level analysis at the subnational level—especially administrative or establishment- or firm-level censuses—and provide a comprehensive mapping and assessment of public programs, intermediary organizations, and regulations. The key contribution of this toolkit, compared with several instruments available in this space, is that it provides an overall framework that is grounded in the microeconomics of an entrepreneur's decisions and provides guidance for implementing the different tasks using the best data available for the country of interest. This helps policy makers design entrepreneurship programs that address specific needs while not losing sight of the broader constraints in the country that affect entrepreneurship outcomes. All survey instruments and implementation guidance for data collection, including surveys for public programs, intermediary organizations, digital market regulations, and start-ups, are available online.

Defining the type of entrepreneurship

Defining the focus of entrepreneurship activity is key for setting policy priorities. Table I.2 describes the heterogeneity involved in entrepreneurship and entrepreneurs. Three common variables used by policy makers for discussing or targeting interventions aiming to boost entrepreneurship are age (for example, start-ups), size (for example, microbusinesses and SMEs)—including changes in size over time (for example, high-growth firms)—and sector (for example, manufacturing). In most cases, these are not exclusive categories. A firm can be a start-up (new) of any size or sector and achieve high growth. Very often, however, the term *start-up* is used to refer to a specific subsample of these new and young firms; the firms in this subsample are usually looking to scale up quickly

TABLE I.1 Comparison of major entrepreneurship ecosystem assessment approaches

ATTRIBUTE	INSTRUMENT			
	GEM	STARTUP GENOME	GLOBAL ENTREPRENEURSHIP INDEX	OECD SME AND ENTREPRENEURSHIP OUTLOOK[a]
Organization	Global Entrepreneurship Research Organization	Startup Genome	Global Entrepreneurship and Development Institute	OECD
Geographic coverage	Global	Three hundred ecosystems in 56 countries	Global	Thirty-eight OECD member countries
Extent of coverage of ecosystem aspects	Perspective and characteristics of individual entrepreneurs (both existing and intentional) Expert opinions on ecosystem aspects such as policies, financing, education, market openness	Clusters of start-ups and related entities that reside within a 100-kilometer radius (typically big cities) Quantitative measures of ecosystem aspects, including performance, funding, market reach, connectedness, experience and talent, and knowledge	Country-level ecosystem aspects covered by several variables, including internet usage, market agglomeration, business risk, economic freedom, and depth of capital market	SMEs and entrepreneurs, including some ecosystem indicators as mentioned below (for example, regulatory framework, skills availability)
Pillars and dimensions	1. Social, cultural, political, and economic context 2. Social values toward entrepreneurship 3. Individual attributes 4. Entrepreneurial activity 5. Entrepreneurial outputs (new jobs, new value-added) 6. Outcomes (socioeconomic development)	For the ranking of ecosystems: six dimensions with several indicators: 1. Performance (for example, start-up valuations) 2. Funding 3. Market reach (for example, access to large companies) 4. Connectedness (for example, number of meetup groups) 5. Experience and talent (for example, number of coders) 6. Knowledge (for example, patents)	Fourteen pillars across three dimensions: 1. Attitudes (for example, opportunity perception, risk acceptance) 2. Abilities (for example, technology absorption, human capital) 3. Aspirations (for example, product innovation, risk capital) For each dimension, the data cover institutional and individual variables.	Factors of SME&E structural vulnerability (for example, size of SMEs and self-employed population, exposure to lockdowns and disruptions in global value chains) Sources of SME&E resilience (for example, digital uptake, access to liquidity, skills availability, entrepreneurship regulatory framework)
Methodology and data sources	Two surveys: 1. Adult Population Survey: Representative samples of the adult population for every economy 2. National Expert Survey: Expert survey for every economy Desk research	1. Desk research 2. Expert interviews 3. Survey of more than 10,000 founders and start-up executives 4. Data from proprietary sources like Crunchbase 5. Data from local partners (accelerators, incubators)	Secondary data sources (official statistics, academic research, existing indexes, and survey data, GEM survey)	Secondary data sources (including from OECD, World Bank, national statistics, GEM survey)

Sources: GEDI, n.d.; GEM, n.d.; OECD 2021; Startup Genome 2022.

Note: This table provides an overall summary of these initiatives. For more details, please consult the original indexes and methodology. GEM = Global Entrepreneurship Monitor; OECD = Organisation for Economic Co-operation and Development; SMEs = small and medium enterprises; SME&E = small and medium enterprises and entrepreneurship.

a. The OECD has used different methodologies to assess entrepreneurship. The one summarized in this table refers to the methodology used in OECD (2021) but is not available as time series data.

TABLE I.2 Types of entrepreneurial firms

TYPE	AGE	SIZE	SECTOR	CHARACTERISTICS
Microbusinesses	Any	<5 employees	Any	Mostly subsistence or necessity entrepreneurs with potentially low growth prospects
Small and medium enterprises	Any	5–249 employees	Any	Heterogeneous group of firms defined according to their size, as measured by either employees or revenue
High-growth firms	>3 years	Any	Any	Firms that start with at least 10 employees and grow revenue or number of employees by more than 20 percent per year for three years (OECD definition)
Start-ups	≤5 years	Any	Any	Heterogeneous group of new firms
Tech start-ups and high-potential start-ups	≤5 years	Any	Any, but likely digital	New businesses looking to scale up quickly using technology and new business models, mostly with an explicit high-growth intent driven by a winner-take-all environment

Source: Original table for this publication.

Note: OECD = Organisation for Economic Co-operation and Development.

using intensive technologies or new business models. Another dimension commonly used is informality, which is more prevalent among microbusinesses.

Digital entrepreneurship, tech start-ups, and new business models

Digital solutions are expected to become even more important in the context of the post-COVID-19 pandemic. The success of tech companies agglomerated around areas such as Silicon Valley has spread widely the view that this is what entrepreneurial ecosystems are about. Indeed, this is an extraordinary example of a successful ecosystem, but entrepreneurial ecosystems are not restricted to digital (or high-tech) business, nor are the conditions replicable in other regions or sectors. However, local digital entrepreneurship can play an important role in facilitating the diffusion and adaptation of digital solutions in many other sectors and regions, helping traditional businesses to become more digitalized to bring wider economic benefits beyond the digital start-ups themselves. Modules 3 and 5 of this toolkit provide some database and survey tools with which to examine the unique challenges and needs of digital entrepreneurs.

Female-led entrepreneurship

Women entrepreneurs tend to encounter barriers to their economic participation that differ from those of their male counterparts—either in degree or in nature. Male and female entrepreneurs operate in the same ecosystem and thus may encounter the same problems related to, for example, accessing finance and markets, the legal and regulatory environment, or insufficient information. However, these problems are often more pronounced for women because of factors such as restrictive social norms, care and household burdens, and unequal treatment under the law. In addition, women entrepreneurs may face obstacles that are virtually nonexistent for their male counterparts, for example, restricted mobility, limitations due to pregnancy and childbirth, and laws that actively discriminate against women.

To gain a nuanced view of an entrepreneurial ecosystem that takes into account gender-specific challenges, one can add a "gender lens" to the analysis. The World Bank has developed a methodology that provides thorough diagnostic processes to unearth key constraints to female entrepreneurship in a given ecosystem: "Using Digital Solutions to Address Barriers to Female Entrepreneurship."[7] This resource is a practical guide to identifying constraints (and their underlying causes) faced by women entrepreneurs, and to designing innovative interventions to ease constraints, with a focus on digitally enabled activities.

NOTES

1. An extensive literature provides different concepts and approaches to the term *entrepreneurial ecosystem* (Audretsch et al. 2019; Isenberg 2010).
2. "[A] biological ecosystem is a complex set of relationships among the living resources, habitats, and residents of an area, whose functional goal is to maintain an [energy] equilibrium sustaining state" (Jackson 2011, 1).
3. Some of these failures can be government failures or inefficiencies created by interventions of the government itself (for example, distortive regulations).
4. The mobility costs faced by workers across sectors and regions are well documented in the literature (Artuç, Chaudhuri, and McLaren 2010; Dix-Carneiro 2014).
5. Many of the needed interventions are related to knowledge that is more likely to be diffused in a local ecosystem.
6. These indicators have been widely available in Organisation for Economic Co-operation and Development (OECD) countries through the OECD publication *Entrepreneurship at a Glance* (for example, OECD 2017). They have been much less widely available in non-OECD countries.
7. See https://digitalforwomen.worldbank.org/sites/gender_toolkit/themes/barrier/pdf /Toolkit-v2.pdf.

REFERENCES

Acs, Z. J., E. Autio, and L. Szerb. 2014. "National Systems of Entrepreneurship: Measurement Issues and Policy Implications." *Research Policy* 43 (3): 476–94.

Acs, Z. J., E. Stam, D. B. Audretsch, and A. O'Connor. 2017. "The Lineages of the Entrepreneurial Ecosystem Approach." *Small Business Economics* 49 (1): 1–10.

Akhlaque, Asya, Shawn Weiming Tan, Tingting Juni Zhu, and Philip Grinsted. 2022. "Digital Market Regulations for Promoting Business Innovation and Digitalization in Vietnam." World Bank Group, Washington, DC. https://documents1.worldbank.org/curated /en/099755006152227000/pdf/P1595780ec45e20bf09f6308da9d054ef29.pdf.

Andrews, R. J., C. Fazio, J. Guzman, Y. Liu, and S. Stern. 2022. "The Startup Cartography Project: Measuring and Mapping Entrepreneurial Ecosystems." *Research Policy* 51 (2): 104437.

Artuç, Erhan, Shubham Chaudhuri, and John McLaren. 2010. "Trade Shocks and Labor Adjustment: A Structural Empirical Approach." *American Economic Review* 100 (3): 1008–45. https://doi.org/10.1257/aer.100.3.1008.

Audretsch, D. B., and M. Belitski. 2021. "Towards an Entrepreneurial Ecosystem Typology for Regional Economic Development: The Role of Creative Class and Entrepreneurship." *Regional Studies* 55 (4): 735–56.

Audretsch, D. B., M. Belitski, and N. Cherkas. 2021. "Entrepreneurial Ecosystems in Cities: The Role of Institutions." *PLOS One* 16 (3): e0247609.

Audretsch, David B., M. Cruz, and J. Torres. 2022. "Revisiting Entrepreneurial Ecosystems." Policy Research Working Paper 10229, World Bank, Washington, DC. http://documents .worldbank.org/curated/en/099413211142227958/IDU04c1d171703fac0466a083eb0 c835a900e26d.

Audretsch, David B., James A. Cunningham, Donald F. Kuratko, Erik E. Lehmann, and Matthias Menter. 2019. "Entrepreneurial Ecosystems: Economic, Technological, and Societal Impacts." *Journal of Technology Transfer* 44 (2): 313–25. https://doi.org/10.1007/s10961-018-9690-4.

Autio, E., and J. Levie. 2017. "Management of Entrepreneurial Ecosystems." In *The Wiley Handbook of Entrepreneurship*, edited by Gorkan Ahmetoglu, Tomas Chamorro-Premuzic, Bailey Klinger, and Tessa Karcisky, 423–49. Hoboken, NJ: Wiley Blackwell.

Cao, Z., and X. Shi. 2021. "A Systematic Literature Review of Entrepreneurial Ecosystems in Advanced and Emerging Economies." *Small Business Economics* 57 (1): 75–110.

Cirera, Xavier, and William F. Maloney. 2017. *The Innovation Paradox: Developing-Country Capabilities and the Unrealized Promise of Technological Catch-Up*. Washington, DC: World Bank.

Correa, Paulo. 2014. "Public Expenditure Reviews in Science, Technology, and Innovation: A Guidance Note." Report 93076, World Bank, Washington, DC.

Cruz, Marcio, Mark A. Dutz, and Carlos Rodríguez-Castelán. 2022. *Digital Senegal for Inclusive Growth: Technological Transformation for Better and More Jobs*. International Development in Focus. Washington, DC: World Bank. http://hdl.handle.net/10986/36860.

Cruz, Marcio, and Zenaida Hernandez Uriz. 2022. "Entrepreneurship Ecosystems and MSMEs in Kenya: Strengthening Businesses in the Aftermath of the Pandemic." World Bank, Washington, DC. https://doi.org/10.1596/38230.

Cruz, Marcio, Natasha Kapil, Pablo Andres Astudillo Estevez, Christopher David Haley, Zoe Cordelia Lu, and Pelin Arslan. 2022. "Starting Up Romania: Entrepreneurship Ecosystem Diagnostic." World Bank, Washington, DC. https://doi.org/10.1596/37564.

De Morán, Mayra, Pedro Andres Amo, Marcio Cruz, Gabriela Montenegro, Jesica Torres, Kati Suominen, Aarre Laakso, Nataly Lovo, and Juan Francisco González. 2021. "Digital Entrepreneurship and Innovation in Central America." Washington, DC: International Finance Corporation, World Bank Group. https://www.ifc.org/content/dam/ifc/doc/mgrt/digital-entrepreneurship-and-innovation-in-central-america.pdf.

Dix-Carneiro, Rafael. 2014. "Trade Liberalization and Labor Market Dynamics." *Econometrica* 82 (3): 825–85. https://doi.org/10.3982/ECTA10457.

GEDI (Global Entrepreneurship and Development Institute). n.d. Washington, DC. http://thegedi.org/tool/.

GEM (Global Entrepreneurship Monitor). n.d. London, UK. https://www.gemconsortium.org/.

Guzman, J., and S. Stern. 2020. "The State of American Entrepreneurship: New Estimates of the Quantity and Quality of Entrepreneurship for 32 US States, 1988–2014." *American Economic Journal: Economic Policy* 12 (4): 212–43.

Isenberg, Daniel J. 2010. "How to Start an Entrepreneurial Revolution." *Harvard Business Review* 88 (6): 40–50.

Isenberg, Daniel J. 2016. "Applying the Ecosystem Metaphor to Entrepreneurship: Uses and Abuses." *Antitrust Bulletin* 61 (4): 564–73.

Jackson, Deborah J. 2011. "What Is an Innovation Ecosystem?" National Science Foundation, Arlington, VA.

Lasagabaster Latorre, Maria Esperanza, Ernesto Lopez-Córdova, Jesica Torres Coronado, Eduardo Piedra Gonzalez, Horman Millán, and Martha Peña Ceniceros. 2023. "Mexico—Entrepreneurship Ecosystem Diagnostic." Washington, DC: World Bank. https://documents1.worldbank.org/curated/en/099051623222013781/pdf/P177889077ff4b0f80b42d01ccdb32cd07e.pdf.

Leendertse, J., M. Schrijvers, and E. Stam. 2021. "Measure Twice, Cut Once: Entrepreneurial Ecosystem Metrics." *Research Policy* 50: 104336.

Maloney, W. F. 2017. "Revisiting the National Innovation System in Developing Countries." Policy Research Working Paper 8219, World Bank, Washington, DC.

Moore, J. F. 1993. "Predators and Prey: A New Ecology of Competition." *Harvard Business Review* 71 (3): 75–86.

O'Connor, A., and D. Audretsch. 2022. "Regional Entrepreneurial Ecosystems: Learning from Forest Ecosystems." *Small Business Economics* 60: 1051–79.

OECD (Organisation for Economic Co-operation and Development). 2017. *Entrepreneurship at a Glance 2017*. Paris: OECD Publishing. http://dx.doi.org/10.1787/entrepreneur_aag-2017-en.

OECD (Organisation for Economic Co-operation and Development). 2021. *OECD SME and Entrepreneurship Outlook 2021*. Paris: OECD Publishing. https://doi.org/10.1787/97a5bbfe-en.

Stam, E. 2015. "Entrepreneurial Ecosystems and Regional Policy: A Sympathetic Critique." *European Planning Studies* 23 (9): 1759–69.

Stam, E., and A. Van de Ven. 2021. "Entrepreneurial Ecosystem Elements." *Small Business Economics* 56 (2): 809–32.

Startup Genome. 2022. "The Global Startup Ecosystem Report 2022." https://startupgenome .com/reports/gser2022.

Szerb, L., E. Lafuente, K. Horváth, and B. Páger. 2019. "The Relevance of Quantity and Quality Entrepreneurship for Regional Performance: The Moderating Role of the Entrepreneurial Ecosystem." *Regional Studies* 53 (9): 1308–20.

White, Justine, Toni Kristian Eliasz, Tingting Juni Zhu, Ana Paula Cusolito, Philip Grinsted, Hangyul Song, Sara Nyman, Claudia Garcia Gonzalez, Nicolas Friederici, Wycliff Tlhalefang Moeletsi, and Ganesh Rasagam. 2022. "South Africa—Private Digital Platform Assessment (English)." World Bank Group, Washington, DC. https://documents1.worldbank .org/curated/en/099060723023040194/pdf/P1718550a6e9010570be020c4853b34846e .pdf.

Wurth, B., E. Stam, and B. Spigel. 2021. "Toward an Entrepreneurial Ecosystem Research Program." *Entrepreneurship Theory and Practice* 45 (3).

Zhu, Tingting Juni, Philip Grinsted, Hangyul Song, and Malathi Velamuri. 2022. "A Spiky Digital Business Landscape: What Can Developing Countries Do?" World Bank, Washington, DC. https://elibrary.worldbank.org/doi/abs/10.1596/39437.

Zottel, Siegfried, Tingting Juni Zhu, Ana Cristina Alonso Soria, and Yoon Keongmin. 2021. "Regulatory Analysis: Digital Entrepreneurship in Nigeria." World Bank Group, Washington, DC. https://documents1.worldbank.org/curated/en/099062823151013200/pdf /P167399088635b0260b2e3061ffffaf10f6.pdf.

1 Context

Cross-Country Context Analysis

1.1 INTRODUCTION

The cross-country context analysis provides a snapshot of the entrepreneurial ecosystem by assessing performance outputs and ecosystem pillars across countries. The key deliverable of this stage is the country snapshot report, which can provide a general overview of the ecosystem and identify gaps at an aggregate level. It provides the baseline for further entrepreneurial ecosystem analysis, taking into consideration output indicators as well as associated inputs from the ecosystem pillars. In particular, it identifies cross-cutting factors that affect firms and entrepreneurs across sectors or regions. It concludes with a summary of strengths and challenges for entrepreneurship.[1]

This module aims to address three questions through a cross-country perspective:

- What is the entrepreneurship performance of the country as measured in three key dimensions: entry and exit of firms, scaling up, and innovating?
- What are the initial supply and demand conditions of the entrepreneurial ecosystem pillars at the country level?
- What are the key financial, regulatory, and cultural barriers to improving the allocation of resources toward impactful entrepreneurship?

A sample structure for module 1 is provided in box 1.1.

The selection of peer countries is a precondition for conducting the cross-country analysis. The purpose of reviewing peer countries is to gain an understanding of a country's progression along its development path, place its outcomes in context, and establish a benchmark against which its relative performance can be assessed. It is often useful to consider two types of peers: (1) structural and (2) aspirational. Structural peers are countries with economic characteristics and overall outcomes similar to the one being analyzed. Aspirational peers possess similar structural conditions but have evolved and performed better than the country in question. More details on how to select peers are given in box 1.2.

Box 1.1

Country context analysis: Proposed structure

A. Introduction
B. The universe of firms
C. Entrepreneurship outputs

   1. Entrepreneurship dynamics (entry and exit of firms)
   2. Impactful entrepreneurship (scale up and innovation)

D. Ecosystem pillars assessment

   1. Supply-side factors: Physical capital, human capital, and knowledge capital
   2. Demand-side factors: Firm capabilities, incentives to invest and accumulate, entrepreneurial characteristics
   3. Barriers to accumulation: Access to finance, regulations, social capital, and culture

E. Strengths and challenges for entrepreneurship (summary of key findings)

Box 1.2

Selecting peer countries

Outlining a clear set of criteria for the selection of peers is crucial, given the sensitivity of many stakeholders to the set of countries that are considered peers. Hence, it is important to reach consensus on the peer countries before any results are presented.

Country teams should be guided by their knowledge of the binding issues and combine that with a data-led approach. Normally, the selection criteria will be based on a combination of important determinants, including geographic proximity, size, economic development, and economic composition. Further, peers can also be chosen from among standard groups, such as commodity exporters, island states, small states, low-income countries, fragile countries, and so forth.

There are also two standard World Bank tools for a more formal peer selection process:

1. The *Dynamic Benchmarking* tool is a Stata tool that helps users identify structural and aspirational peers based on a uniform and objective formula that can be applied to an infinite number of criteria and across different periods (up to 2016).

2. *Find My Friends* is an Excel tool that helps identify statistical similarities between countries across the globe, making it easy to compare the development outcomes of a country with those of its relevant peers. The tool instantly identifies where a country is an outlier and allows users to build customized charts with many types of benchmarking.

An additional innovative way to select peers is through propensity score matching and synthetic control methods. Using data on observable characteristics, matching methods can identify countries most similar to the one being analyzed. The synthetic control method constructs a comparison group as a weighted combination of other countries.

Because the purpose of peer countries is not to conduct a comprehensive ranking, it is not necessary to include the full range of possible comparator countries. Further, interpretation can become difficult if too many comparators are included. Hence, four to six countries each for the structural and aspirational peer groups is typical.

Sources: Reis and Farole 2012; World Bank 2019.

1.2 THE UNIVERSE OF FIRMS IN THE COUNTRY

Providing a general overview of the population of firms and their overall characteristics is important in establishing the context and finding comparable data for peer countries. Characterizing the universe of a country's firms is therefore crucial. Further, before delving into the output and ecosystem pillar indicators, the analysis can benefit from first discussing the data sources, data types, and firm demographics within the data set, to provide context. For example, it may be that the data only contain micro, small, and medium enterprises (MSMEs) or have other characteristics that should be kept in mind when interpreting and comparing findings across countries. When working with a subsample of data, it is also helpful to benchmark the general characteristics of the firm population in the available data against known information about the firm universe. This exercise can support the interpretation of results and the extent to which the available data are comparable with those from other countries. Hence, it can be helpful to look at the share of establishments by size, sector, region, formality status, and age, as well as the distribution of employment across firm size groups. An example of such analysis for Kenya is given in box 1.3.

Informality should be given special attention in the description of the universe of firms in developing countries. Many of them have high shares of informal businesses and informal workers. Very frequently, the information on the universe of firms is not updated or even available. Therefore, the analysis must often rely only on formal firms for which data are more commonly available. As a result, the analysis may provide an incomplete picture. Hence, in countries with very high informality, many indicators need to be carefully interpreted, especially if they are aggregated (for example, translated into per capita terms). Providing some information on the extent of informality and the characteristics of the observed formal firms can therefore help the

---

Box 1.3

Setting up the basis for cross-country comparable data

The distribution of firms in the available data and particularly the size and share of formal firms can affect the indicators' interpretation and their cross-country comparability. Therefore, before delving into the results, the analysis should provide this information to the extent possible. As an example, table B1.3.1 shows the number of firms and workers included in the formal and informal data sets used for Kenya, and figure B1.3.1 shows the distribution of firms by size, sector, and age as well as by the distribution of employment by firm size, among formal firms in Kenya. This distribution looks very different when including informal firms.

TABLE B1.3.1 Sources of firm-level data in Kenya

DATABASE	FIRMS	WORKERS
Establishment census—formal businesses	138,190	3.5 million
MSME survey—licensed businesses	1.6 million	6.3 million
MSME survey—unlicensed businesses	5.8 million	8.6 million

Source: KNBS 2017.
Note: Some licensed businesses at the county level could also be formally registered, thus there may be overlaps between the first and second rows. MSME = micro, small, and medium enterprises.

continued

Box 1.3, *continued*

FIGURE B1.3.1

Features of establishments in the Kenyan establishment census

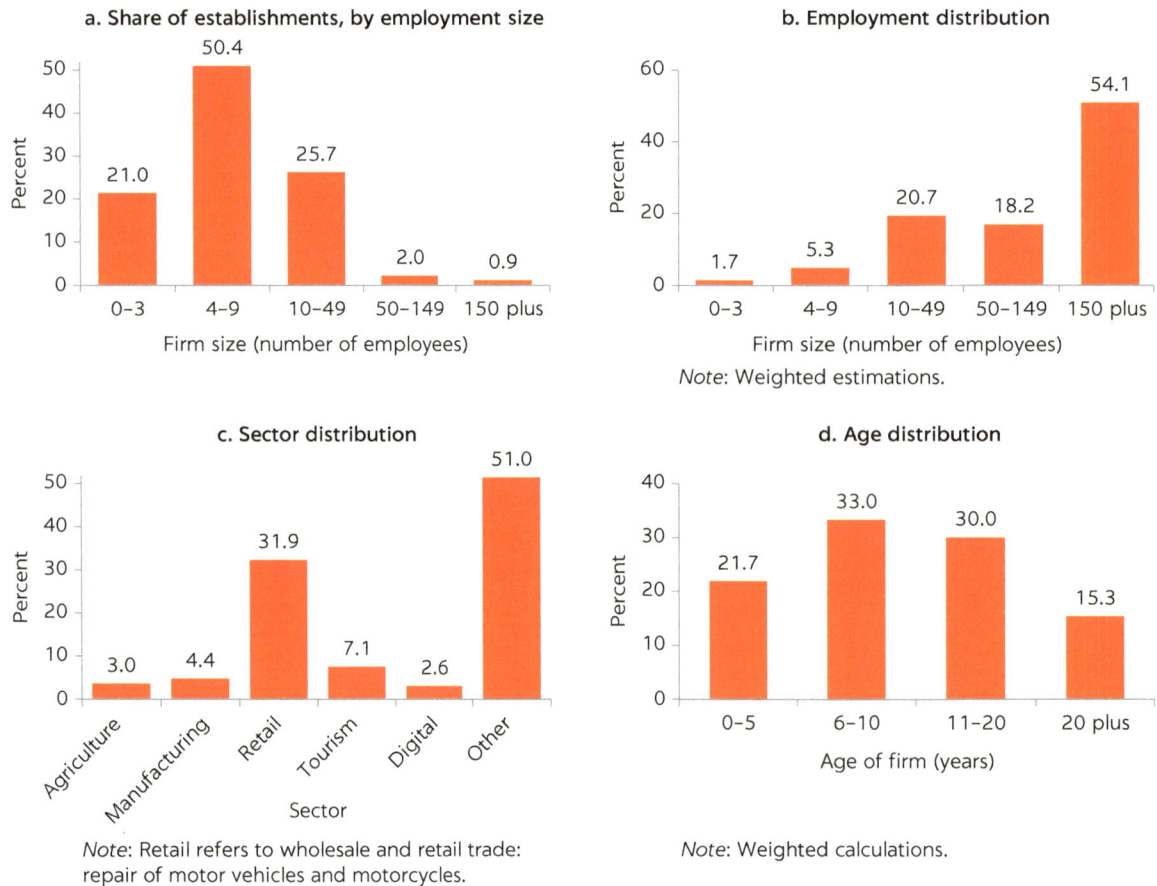

a. Share of establishments, by employment size

b. Employment distribution

Note: Weighted estimations.

c. Sector distribution

d. Age distribution

Note: Retail refers to wholesale and retail trade: repair of motor vehicles and motorcycles.

Note: Weighted calculations.

Sources: Cruz and Hernandez Uriz 2022; KNBS 2017; World Bank Business Pulse Survey 2020.

reader better understand the results. This is particularly important for results referring to the share of firms.[2] Last, cross-country differences in formality should be considered when comparing countries, especially if data on the full universe of firms are unavailable.

It is important, yet challenging, to find firm or establishment census data that can be comparable across countries, particularly in developing economies. The first step is to identify the best available data in the country that can provide the most up-to-date and accurate census of establishments. This information is usually available through national statistical offices and business registries. In some countries, this type of information is also available through administrative data maintained by the ministry of labor or finance. National statistical offices are usually a good starting point for understanding the availability of such data. Surveys based on the available establishment census, such as the World Bank Enterprise Survey, also allow global comparisons of business performance to be made. A good census of firms is also critical as a sample frame for teams that wish to conduct their own surveys. Other data sources that are specific to output and ecosystem pillar indicators are discussed in the following sections.

1.3 ENTREPRENEURSHIP OUTPUTS

Critical outputs of the ecosystem are the rate of business creation (extensive margin) and the rates of business scale up and innovation (intensive margin). Figure 1.1 shows the main output indicators. As shown in table 1.1, these indicators can be divided into two broad groups: (1) entrepreneurship dynamics, capturing the extensive margin, and (2) impactful entrepreneurship, capturing the intensive margin.[3] The first group of indicators aims to uncover the overall entry, exit, and survival dynamics of firms. The impactful entrepreneurship indicators aim to provide additional information on the characteristics and performance variables that are usually associated with a "successful business." These consist of indicators (1) related to firm growth (scaling up) and (2) innovation (upgrading). Even if high-potential enterprises are difficult to identify ahead of time, they are more likely to arise in dynamic ecosystems characterized by high entry rates of better-quality firms, capacity of those firms to scale up, and constant technological upgrading.

The wide variety of indicators available with which to measure entrepreneurship outputs should be selected and tailored to the country's situation. Table 1.1 gives a few examples of potential indicators for each group.[4] It is not an exhaustive list, nor should these variables always be used, because the appropriate

FIGURE 1.1

Entrepreneurship outputs

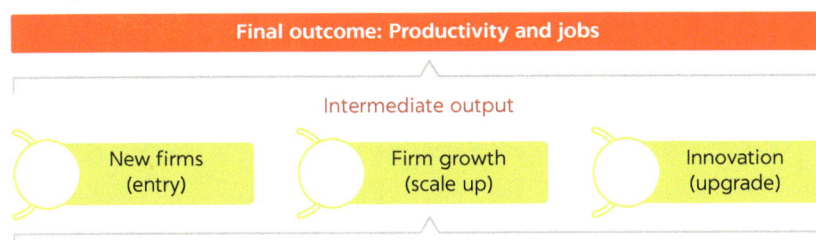

Source: Original figure for this publication.

TABLE 1.1 Indicators to measure entrepreneurship dynamics and impactful entrepreneurship

ENTREPRENEURSHIP DYNAMICS	IMPACTFUL ENTREPRENEURSHIP	
NEW FIRMS (ENTRY)	**FIRM GROWTH (SCALE UP)**	**INNOVATION (UPGRADE)**
INDICATORS		
Density of new businesses relative to GDP per capita	Share of high-growth firms	Share of firms introducing a product or service innovation
Number of new firms relative to population	Average annual employment growth	Share of firms introducing a process innovation
Entry rate of businesses	Average sales or turnover growth	
Exit rate of businesses	Number of workers by firm age group (for example, 20+ years old or less than 5 years old)	Share of firms investing in R&D
Firm survival rate (for example, after one year)	Average productivity and productivity growth	Share of firms using or increasing the use of digital technology
Characteristics of young firms	Share of VC-backed firms	Levels of technology sophistication of firms
DATA SOURCES		
World Bank Entrepreneurship Database	World Bank Enterprise Surveys	World Bank Enterprise Surveys (innovation module)
Firm-level administrative data	Firm-level administrative data	World Bank Firm-level Adoption of Technology Survey[a]
Global Entrepreneurship Monitor		
International Labour Organization		

Source: Original table for this publication.
Note: This table provides examples of indicators, measures, and data sources that can be considered to measure quantity and quality of entrepreneurship output. GDP = gross domestic product; R&D = research and development; VC = venture capital.
a. See Cirera, Comin, and Cruz 2022.

indicators will depend on the country context and data availability. Instead, these examples serve to help teams think about how to assess the entrepreneurship outputs in their context. Taken together, output indicators can serve as proxies to help assess overall performance on entrepreneurship dynamics, growth, and innovation. For example, a low number of workers among very old firms may indicate constraints to scaling up, while few firms backed by venture capital may indicate few high-potential firms. The results of these indicators can be shown in different charts, as, for example, in figure 1.2, analyzing the density

FIGURE 1.2

Entrepreneurship outputs: Example charts

a. Entrepreneurship dynamics: Density of new businesses relative to GDP per capita

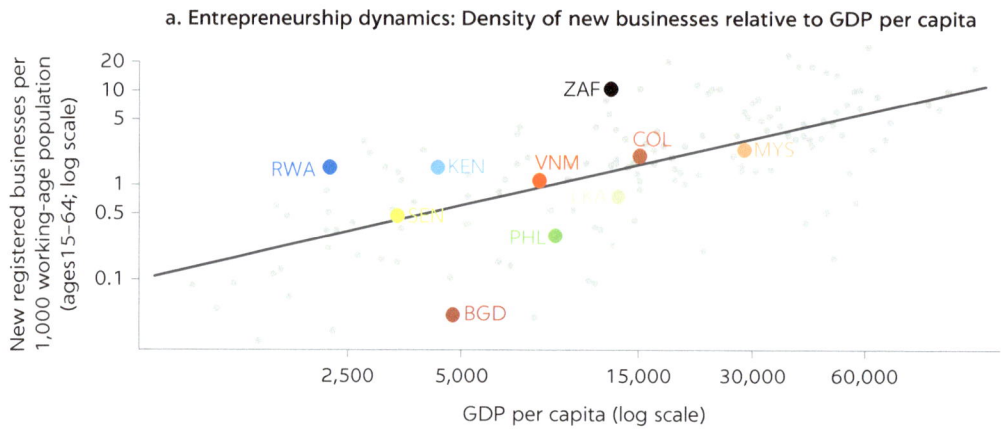

Source: Cruz and Hernandez Uriz 2022. Data sources: World Bank Entrepreneurship Database (World Bank 2023b); World Development Indicators (World Bank 2023c).

Note: For a list of country codes, see https://www.iso.org/obp/ui/#search. GDP = gross domestic product.

b. Scale-up output: Average annual employment growth

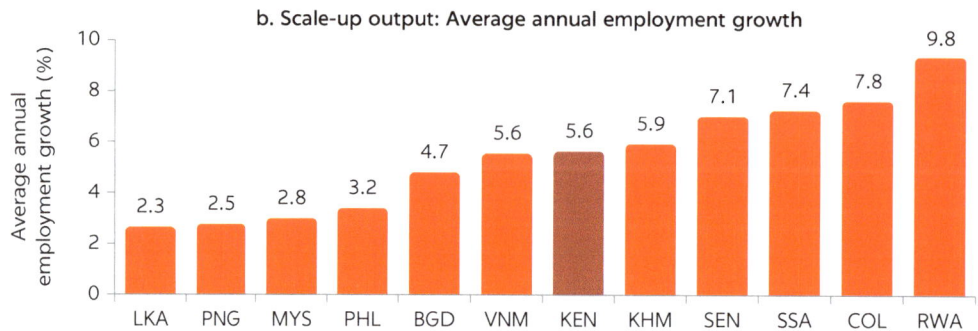

Source: Cruz and Hernandez Uriz 2022. Data source: World Bank Enterprise Survey (World Bank 2023a).

Note: For a list of country codes, see https://www.iso.org/obp/ui/#search.

c. Innovation output: Share of firms that introduced a process innovation

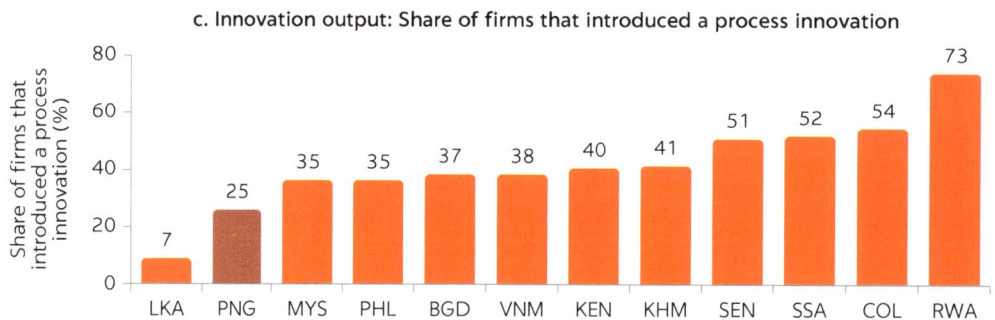

Source: Cruz and Hernandez Uriz 2022. Data source: World Bank Enterprise Survey (World Bank 2023a).

Note: For a list of country codes, see https://www.iso.org/obp/ui/#search.

of new businesses and per capital income (panel a), and comparing Kenya with peer countries, in terms of firm growth (panel b) and innovation (panel c). The choice of charts for the cross-country analysis should be guided by the overall storyline and points deserving emphasis.

There are myriad traditional data sources that are comparable across countries for output variables. Sources of output indicators can include administrative or business registry data. Firm censuses, household surveys, labor surveys, and firm surveys, either custom-made or standard, such as the World Bank Enterprise Survey or the World Bank Firm-level Adoption of Technology Survey, are also valuable data sources. Last, there are many useful cross-country data sets, such as the World Bank World Development Indicators, the Global Innovation Index, the Global Competitiveness Index, and the UNESCO Innovation data set, among others. Table 1.2 highlights some of the strengths and drawbacks of those data sets when analyzing entrepreneurship output from the different dimensions highlighted above.

Nontraditional data collection methods can complement traditional output analysis. Traditional data sources may not always be applicable or able to capture the most recent and complete information on new entrepreneurial activities. Hence, alternative data sources should often be considered, such as web scraping, proprietary data, and merger of traditional data with web-scraped and proprietary data. However, alternative data collection can be especially challenging in many developing countries. Furthermore, it can be challenging to ensure that variables captured in this manner are comparable across countries. An illustration of nontraditional data sources for use in output analysis is given in table 1.3, with more details on implementation in online appendix F.[5] Module 3 presents a global digital business database assembled by the World Bank that uses nontraditional data collection methods to assess digital entrepreneurship, given that tech start-ups are more likely being captured by these web-scraping techniques or by proprietary commercial data sources that serve the venture capital investor community. This database is further cleaned and checked by

TABLE 1.2 Characteristics of data sets available with which to measure entrepreneurship and conduct a cross-country analysis

DATA SOURCE	WHAT IT COVERS	STRENGTHS	LIMITATIONS
World Bank Entrepreneurship Database	Total number of registered firms by country, by year Entry rate and gender entrepreneurship	Large country coverage Informative for entry rate dynamics	Only includes information on number of registered firms
World Bank Enterprise Survey	Representative firm-level survey Covers only formal firms with five or more workers Additional surveys covering informal sector	Cross-country coverage Includes indicators of firm growth and a module on innovation Representative at subnational level	May not include new firms if sampling frame is outdated Small sample size with limited sector stratification for small countries No informal firms in the standard version
World Bank World Development Indicators	Wide variety of aggregate economic measures at the country level	Cross-country coverage Time series (since 1960)	Micro (for example, firm-level) data not available
Global Entrepreneurship Monitor	Surveys of national experts on the entrepreneurship environment and individuals starting a business	Cross-country coverage Coverage of 115 economies since 1999	Many perception-based indicators

Source: Original table for this publication.

TABLE 1.3 Nontraditional data sources for entrepreneurship outputs

CONCEPT	DATA REQUIRED	ALTERNATIVE DATA SOURCES
Entry and exit dynamics of all enterprises in the ecosystem or region (industry level)	Number of new firms	Web scraping of alternative data sources (for example, business directories, Google Places API, Google search results, social media)
		Proprietary sources with company data (for example, PitchBook, Crunchbase)
Number of enterprises with high levels of risk capital (firm level)	Percentage of firms with risk capital	Web scraping of alternative data sources (for example, venture capital directories)
		Proprietary sources with a lot of granular investment data (especially PitchBook, Crunchbase)
		Newspaper data mining to find news announcements about firm funding
Exports and imports or global chain insertion (firm level)	Percentage of firms exporting directly	Proprietary sources with data on trading and exporting companies (especially PitchBook, Crunchbase), based on industry classifications

Source: Original table for this publication.

harmonizing definitions and taxonomies so multiple data sources can be combined and merged. This is particularly important for enlarging the sample size for developing countries that rely on multiple sources of information.

1.4 ENTREPRENEURIAL ECOSYSTEM PILLARS

The three key entrepreneurial ecosystem pillars are (1) resource endowment factors (physical, human, and knowledge capital), (2) firms' demand for resources (market access, firm capabilities, entrepreneur characteristics),[6] and (3) barriers to allocation (access to finance, regulations, social capital). The assessment of the components of the ecosystem pillars is based on the conceptual framework presented in the introduction.

Several potential variables are available with which to assess the components of the ecosystem pillars. Examples of potential indicators for each component are shown in table 1.4. These variables can be considered proxies for the availability or conditions of the factor that should be assessed, but this list is by no means exhaustive. Using such quantifiable indicators is important for identifying where the most binding distortions or constraints lie and thus for guiding policy priorities. Nevertheless, it is important to acknowledge the inevitable limitations of these variables for capturing the overall condition of the ecosystem. An example of potential charts that can be generated from these variables is given in figure 1.3; the charts should be chosen based on the overall storyline and important findings.

Synergies from leveraging both traditional and alternative data sources can provide a clearer picture of the entrepreneurship pillars. Traditional data sources (such as sample surveys and censuses) typically have the advantage of verified and comparable data across countries or regions. Nontraditional data sources complement these by providing access to granular data, filling in the data gaps of traditional sources, and augmenting traditional data. Possible sources for both types of data by input indicator are given in table 1.4. Online appendix F provides more details on the rationale for, implementation of, and bias adjustments in alternative data sources. Currently, however, nontraditional data collection can be especially difficult in many developing countries.

The input indicators to be analyzed should be guided by data availability, data quality, and sometimes correlations between input variables and entrepreneurship outputs. In practice, the availability and quality of data affect which potential indicators can be analyzed. Issues to consider are the lack of

TABLE 1.4 **Suggestive indicators and data sources for assessing the ecosystem pillars**

ECOSYSTEM PILLAR	COMPONENT	INDICATOR	DATA SOURCES FOR DESK WORK
A. SUPPLY FACTORS (INPUTS)	Physical capital and infrastructure	Number of greenfield foreign direct investment projects	fDi Intelligence Database
		Investment flow	Enterprise Survey
		Capital stock (total or per worker)	PENN World Table
		Percentage of population or firms with access to electricity	World Development Indicators
		Percentage of population or firms using the internet	
		Information and communication technology connectivity	
		Number of incubators	
	Human capital	Percentage of working-age population with advanced education (male and female)	Barro-Lee Educational Attainment Dataset
		Availability of scientists and engineers	UNESCO Innovation data set
		Share of science, technology, engineering, and mathematics graduates	ILOSTAT
		Projections on working-age population and educational composition	World Bank Human Capital Index
			Global Innovation Index
		Level of digital skills	World Development Indicators
			UN demographic projections
			IIASA
	Knowledge capital	Top three universities' average QS World University Ranking	QS Ranking
		Gross domestic spending on R&D	Global Innovation Index
		Number of researchers (per population)	Enterprise Survey
		Number of patent applications	UNESCO Innovation data set
		Number of technology extensionists or number of institutions that provide technology extension (weighted by their capacity and quality)	World Intellectual Property Organization
			Global Innovation Index
		Number of mentors	World Development Indicators
		University-industry collaboration in R&D	World Bank Tcdata360
		Collaboration between innovative SMEs and other organizations	
B. DEMAND (FIRMS)	Market access	Mark-up power	World Integrated Trade Solution data
		Average output/input tariff	World Development Indicators
		Herfindahl–Hirschman market concentration index	Global Innovation Index
		External market growth: Total or growth of exported products	Enterprise Survey
		Internal market growth: GDP PPP growth	
		Domestic market scale	
		Percentage of firms exporting directly or indirectly	
		Import content of exports	
		E-commerce (firms selling or individuals buying online)	

continued

TABLE 1.4, *continued*

ECOSYSTEM PILLAR	COMPONENT	INDICATOR	DATA SOURCES FOR DESK WORK
B. DEMAND (FIRMS)	Firm capabilities	Management capabilities	World Management Survey
		Percentage of firms with internationally recognized quality certifications	World Bank Enterprise Survey
		Percentage of firms having their own website	Firm-level Adoption of Technology Survey
		Percentage of firms with an annual financial statement reviewed by external auditors	
		Percentage of firms using technology licensed from foreign companies	
		Percentage of firms adopting digital technologies for general business functions	
		Percentage of firms offering formal training	
	Entrepreneur characteristics	Appetite for entrepreneurial risk	Global Preferences Survey
		Share of entrepreneurs with experience in multinationals or higher education abroad	Enterprise Census
		Education level of entrepreneurs	Global Entrepreneurship Monitor
		Research talent in business enterprise	Global Competitiveness Index
		Entrepreneurial intentions	Global Innovation Index
		Share of necessity versus opportunity entrepreneurship	Household and labor surveys
C. ACCUMULATION AND ALLOCATION BARRIERS	Access to finance	Percentage of firms' loan applications rejected	World Bank Enterprise Survey
		Average lending interest rate	World Development Indicators
		Collateral requirements	Start-up ecosystem assessment in partnership with the Global Entrepreneurship Research Network
		Commercial bank branches (per 100,000 adults)	
		Number of VCs; number of deals from VCs; share of VC lending	
		Domestic credit to the private sector (fraction of GDP)	Global Competitiveness Index
	Regulations	Rigidity of the formal labor market	Institutional Profiles Database
		Governance quality	Worldwide Governance Indicators
		Ease of doing business	
		Average time spent dealing with government regulations	Doing Business
		Time required to start a business	Enterprise Survey
	Social capital and culture	Number of professional associations (lawyers, doctors, and so forth)	Institutional Profiles Database
		Network measures	Start-up ecosystem assessment in partnership with the Global Entrepreneurship Research Network
		Share of women owning a business with more than five employees	
		Fraction of firms where the top manager is a woman	World Values Survey
		Index of social capital	World Bank Tcdata360
		Perception of high-status successful entrepreneurship	

Source: Original table for this publication.

Note: GDP = gross domestic product; IIASA = International Institute for Applied Systems Analysis; PPP = purchasing power parity; R&D = research and development; SMEs = small and medium enterprises; UN = United Nations; UNESCO = United Nations Educational, Scientific, and Cultural Organization; VC = venture capital.

indicators for critical factors, diversity of measures for the same factors, sample coverage, and errors in data collection. To aid in the selection, observing the correlation between output and input variables that are available for the country in question can be helpful, even though these associations cannot be considered causal. For example, table 1.5 shows the correlation between the rate of new business registrations and several indicators for supply, demand,

FIGURE 1.3

Ecosystem pillars: Example charts

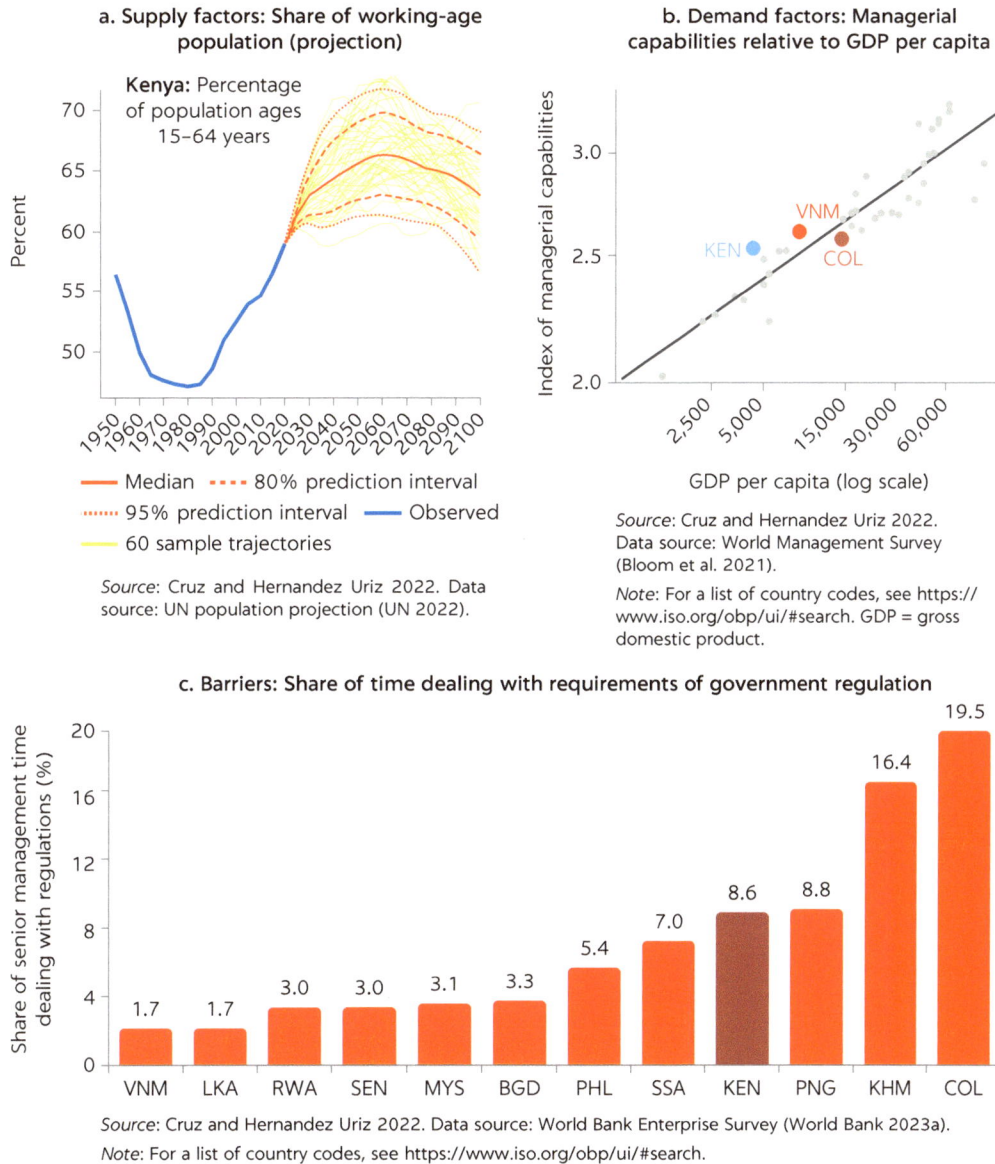

a. Supply factors: Share of working-age population (projection)

Kenya: Percentage of population ages 15–64 years

- Median ···· 80% prediction interval
- ···· 95% prediction interval — Observed
- 60 sample trajectories

Source: Cruz and Hernandez Uriz 2022. Data source: UN population projection (UN 2022).

b. Demand factors: Managerial capabilities relative to GDP per capita

GDP per capita (log scale)

Source: Cruz and Hernandez Uriz 2022. Data source: World Management Survey (Bloom et al. 2021).

Note: For a list of country codes, see https://www.iso.org/obp/ui/#search. GDP = gross domestic product.

c. Barriers: Share of time dealing with requirements of government regulation

VNM 1.7, LKA 1.7, RWA 3.0, SEN 3.0, MYS 3.1, BGD 3.3, PHL 5.4, SSA 7.0, KEN 8.6, PNG 8.8, KHM 16.4, COL 19.5

Source: Cruz and Hernandez Uriz 2022. Data source: World Bank Enterprise Survey (World Bank 2023a).

Note: For a list of country codes, see https://www.iso.org/obp/ui/#search.

and barriers using cross-country regressions. Table 1.5 presents the correlation between indicators proposed to be used as proxies in the entrepreneurial ecosystem pillars and the new-business density indicator across countries. Overall, these indicators are correlated with new business entry in the direction expected by the conceptual framework, informed by a theoretical model. However, these correlations do not imply a causal relationship.

The analysis in table 1.5 is based on public cross-country data where information for Kenya is available. Statistically significant variables show that they are strongly associated with the entrepreneurship outputs, but again, this is not evidence of a causal relationship. Evidence of a causal relationship between some of these factors and entrepreneurship output can be found with a careful review of the literature—some references are provided in module 6—which is important to inform and support the analysis.

TABLE 1.5 Cross-country correlation matrix of output and entrepreneurial ecosystem pillar components

		OUTPUTS		
PILLAR	COMPONENT	NEW BUSINESS DENSITY PER 1,000 WORKING-AGE PEOPLE (POOLING)	NEW BUSINESS DENSITY PER 1,000 WORKING-AGE PEOPLE (CROSS-SECTION)	NEW BUSINESS DENSITY PER 1,000 WORKING-AGE PEOPLE (PANEL FE)
Supply	Stock of capital per engaged person	0.635***	0.033***	1.472***
	Fraction of the population using the internet	0.651***	−0.021	0.013***
	Share of graduates in science and engineering in total tertiary graduates	0.05	0.077***	0.010**
	Share of working-age population with advanced education	0.191***	0.228	−0.002
	Score of the top three universities' average ranking	0.209***	0.463***	0.067
	Number of researchers per million people	0.519***	−0.056	0.443***
Demand	Domestic market scale	−0.039	0.159	0.407***
	Percentage of firms exporting directly or indirectly (at least 1 percent of sales)	0.397***	0.010	0.019
	Research talent in business enterprise	0.133*	0.069	−0.002
	Percentage of firms with internationally recognized quality certification	0.349***	2.684**	0.005
	Managerial capabilities	0.451**	0.015***	0.000
	Appetite for entrepreneurial risk (perceived; scale 1–7)	0.250***	−0.070***	0.547
Barriers	Domestic credit to the private sector (fraction of GDP)	0.476***	0.131	0.004
	Average lending interest rate	−0.271***	−0.608***	−0.026***
	Fraction of senior management time dealing with requirements	0.113	4.155***	0.032*
	Time required to start a business (days)	−0.350***	−0.083	−0.275***
	Index of social capital (scale 0–100)	0.353***	0.033***	1.407***
	Fraction of firms in which top manager is a woman	0.05	−0.021	0.002

Source: Cruz and Hernandez Uriz 2022.
Note: The results provide the coefficients of regression analysis. Variables that are not shares or growth rates are in log. Results are based on panel data (2006–20). FE = fixed effects; GDP = gross domestic product.
***p<0.01, **p<0.05, *p<0.1

1.5 STRENGTHS AND CHALLENGES FOR ENTREPRENEURSHIP

The cross-country analysis will provide a set of strengths and weaknesses related to entrepreneurship dynamics and impactful entrepreneurship, thereby setting the stage for further investigation of policy direction. When summarizing the results, it is important to minimize the focus on the variables themselves, because they are simply proxies. Rather, teams should focus on the bigger picture regarding the constraints revealed by the combination of indicators. An example of such a summary is given in table 1.6, which shows that the analyzed country is generating new entry of firms (high entrepreneurship rate), but struggles with quality, that is, the main constraint is impactful entrepreneurship. The same can be done for each of the nine input components that fall under the pillars of supply, demand, and barriers, as shown in table 1.7.

TABLE 1.6 Example summary of main strengths and challenges of entrepreneurship outputs

ENTREPRENEURSHIP OUTPUT	STRENGTHS	CHALLENGES
Entry	New firm creation, consistent across age groups and gender	Low proportion of young firms, indicating low survival rates despite high firm creation
		Necessity entrepreneurship dominant because of lack of economic opportunities
Scaling up	High share of firms achieving high growth	Low employment growth
		Low levels of workers in older firms
	Larger firm size in old cohorts	Limited number of high-growth firms
Innovation	High R&D spending	Low levels of R&D outputs and product innovation
	State-of-the-art automotive sector	Low levels of process innovations
		Underemphasis on private sector–led innovation

Source: Original table for this publication.
Note: R&D = research and development.

TABLE 1.7 Example summary of main strengths and challenges of entrepreneurship pillars

ENTREPRENEURSHIP PILLAR	COMPONENTS OF PILLAR	STRENGTHS	CHALLENGES
Supply	Physical capital and infrastructure	Access to electricity	Low stock of capital
		Uptake of firm-level information and communication technology usage during COVID-19 (coronavirus)	Limited transport infrastructure
	Human capital	Stock of science and engineering graduates	Mismatch of skills
		Quality of graduates' skills	Brain drain
	Knowledge capital	University-industry research collaboration	Few researchers
		Research and development expenditure	Average ranking of universities
Demand	Access to markets	Access to European Union markets	Distortive effect of taxes and subsidies on competition
			Domestic market scale
	Firm capabilities	Managerial capabilities	International quality certifications
		Technology licensed from foreign companies	
	Entrepreneurial characteristics	Appetite for entrepreneurial risk	Appetite for disruptive ideas
Barriers	Access to finance	Lending rates	Loan rejection rates
		Financial sector depth	Collateral requirements
	Regulations	Legal framework's adaptability to digital business models	Legal framework not optimized for digital start-ups
			Lack of regulations to encourage venture capital investments and crowdfunding
	Social capital and culture	Entrepreneurship enjoys reasonably high social status	Limited generalized interpersonal trust

Source: Based on Cruz et al. 2021.

NOTES

1. The figures and tables presented in this module are illustrative examples extracted from the pilots implemented in Kenya (Cruz and Hernandez Uriz 2022) and Romania (Cruz et al. 2021). For further details about the results, please consult the references.
2. The denominator of the share may not represent all firms, but only all formal firms, which can be misleading.

3. The extensive margin refers to the decision of whether to enter entrepreneurship, whereas the intensive margin corresponds to measures of performance once the business has entered entrepreneurship.

4. A further source of potential variables is the OECD-Eurostat Entrepreneurship Indicators Programme and the Kauffman Indicators of Entrepreneurship.

5. Online appendixes A through F are available at https://openknowledge.worldbank.org /handle/10986/40305.

6. This description aims to capture some features leading the demand for resources by new entrepreneurs, incumbent firms, and output markets. The firm capabilities component aims to characterize the type of demand for resources from incumbent firms. Entrepreneur characteristics aim to identify the relevant type of entrepreneurs in the ecosystem. If data are available, it is useful to differentiate changes over time to identify the profile of new entrepreneurs.

REFERENCES

Bloom, Nicholas, Renata Lemos, Raffaella Sadun, Daniela Scur, and John Van Reenen. 2021. "World Management Survey—Manufacturing." https://doi.org/10.7910/DVN/OY6CBK.

Cirera, Xavier, Diego Comin, and Marcio Cruz. 2022. *Bridging the Technological Divide: Technology Adoption by Firms in Developing Countries*. Washington, DC: World Bank.

Cruz, Marcio, and Zenaida Hernandez Uriz. 2022. *Entrepreneurship Ecosystems and MSMEs in Kenya: Strengthening Businesses in the Aftermath of the Pandemic*. Washington, DC: World Bank. https://elibrary.worldbank.org/doi/abs/10.1596/38230.

Cruz, Marcio, Natasha Kapil, Pablo Andres Astudillo Estevez, Christopher David Haley, Zoe Cordelia Lu, and Pelin Arslan. 2021. *Starting Up Romania: Entrepreneurship Ecosystem Diagnostic*. Washington, DC: World Bank Group. http://documents.worldbank.org/curated /en/099920106072238493/P174325083a5cc0eb090350dcde4c6a32df.

KNBS (Kenya National Bureau of Statistics). 2017. "Census of Establishments 2017." January 31, 2017. https://www.knbs.or.ke/census-of-establishments-2017/.

Reis, José Guilherme, and Thomas Farole. 2012. *Trade Competitiveness Diagnostic Toolkit*. Washington, DC: World Bank. https://elibrary.worldbank.org/doi/abs/10.1596/978 -0-8213-8937-9.

UN (United Nations). 2022. "World Population Prospects 2022." United Nations Department of Economic and Social Affairs, Population Division, New York. https://population.un.org /wpp/.

World Bank. 2019. "CEM 2.0 Country Scan Guidelines." Macroeconomics, Trade & Investment. Third Version. World Bank, Washington, DC.

World Bank. 2023a. "Enterprise Surveys." Enterprise Surveys Indicators Data. World Bank, Washington, DC. https://www.enterprisesurveys.org/en/enterprisesurveys.

World Bank. 2023b. World Bank Entrepreneurship Database. World Bank, Washington, DC. https://www.worldbank.org/en/programs/entrepreneurship.

World Bank. 2023c. "World Development Indicators." World Bank, Washington, DC. https://datatopics.worldbank.org/world-development-indicators/.

Assessing Local Entrepreneurial Ecosystems

2.1 INTRODUCTION

A national overview of the outputs and pillars of entrepreneurial ecosystems is critical, but these ecosystems are localized phenomena. The analysis of the aggregate entrepreneurial ecosystems in the previous module helps identify critical barriers and provides a "big picture." However, a country could be home to several local ecosystems of varied depth and sophistication—for example, subsistence micro-businesses, tech start-ups, spinoffs from large companies—and varied sectoral focuses.

Local entrepreneurial ecosystems are inextricably linked with the surrounding environment. Identifying potential entrepreneurial ecosystems and assessing the components of their pillars at the local level are important prerequisites for designing effective and well-targeted policies. Because economic activity is often spatially correlated, the same interventions can have significantly different results in different geographic locations. Similarly, the growth potential of different local ecosystems can vary and may require different policy interventions. Therefore, targeting interventions to local environments and specific sectors can provide a higher possibility of good outcomes. Subnational analysis provides policy makers with an in-depth look at successful ecosystems in their regions or countries so they can experiment with targeted interventions that can be implemented on a broader scale.

This module aims to address five questions through a subnational perspective. A sample structure for module 2 is provided in box 2.1.[1]

- How is economic activity distributed regionally within the country?
- Which are the most important or technology-intensive regional ecosystems?
- What are the key characteristics of start-ups?
- What are the key obstacles reported by start-ups?
- How connected are the local entrepreneurial ecosystems?

Box 2.1

Subnational analysis: Proposed structure

A. Describe the regional landscape of firms and entrepreneurial ecosystems.

B. Identify the potential of the local entrepreneurial ecosystem.

1. For industry A
2. For industry B
3. For subsequent industries
4. Summary of local ecosystems

C. Describe entrepreneurship characteristics and performance across subnational ecosystems.

1. Outputs
2. Ecosystem input components
3. Main obstacles faced by entrepreneurs
4. The demand for policies
5. Summary

D. Provide a deep dive into a local ecosystem using start-up survey data.

2.2 IDENTIFYING LOCAL ENTREPRENEURIAL ECOSYSTEMS

To identify local ecosystems, the diversity and quality of geographic agglomerations of firms across key sectors or value chains can be evaluated using firm census data. Focusing on a few broad strategic sectors based on government priorities or the country's economic structure and potential is useful. For example, agribusiness, tourism, retail, digital, knowledge-intensive services, high-tech manufacturing, and light manufacturing are often sectors receiving the most attention. The firm census is the ideal data set for this analysis because it contains the relevant variables for all the firms in a country.

The methodology proposed in this module for measuring diversity uses a variety of indicators that are correlated across regions. Diversity is a key component for entrepreneurship and innovation. It indicates how varied the productive knowledge base in a region is and is strongly associated with increased output, productivity, and growth (Karlsson, Rickardsson, and Wincent 2021). To measure diversity, the methodology first looks for statistically significant agglomerations of subnational geographic units (such as regions) with a high density of establishments within each 4-digit subsector in the broad strategic sector. It then counts the number of subsectors for which a region (or district or county) is part of an agglomeration. If data at the 4-digit level are not available, the 3- or 2-digit level can be used. Panel a of map 2.1 provides an example of diversity agglomerations from Senegal's agribusiness value chain.

Similarly, to capture quality, the methodology looks for agglomerations in measures of business dynamism and potential for additional growth within a sector. The quality indicators can include the share or number of young firms, large firms (by number of workers and by turnover), high-performance firms, high-growth firms,[2] new firms, formal firms, firms where the manager has tertiary education, as well as entry and survival rates (for example, after three years). The aggregate measure of quality then counts the number of quality indicators for which a region (or district or county) is part of an agglomeration. Map 2.1, panel b, provides an example of quality agglomerations from Senegal's agribusiness value chain. Further details on the methodology are provided in box 2.2.

MAP 2.1

Identifying diversity and quality in agglomerations in Senegal's agribusiness sector

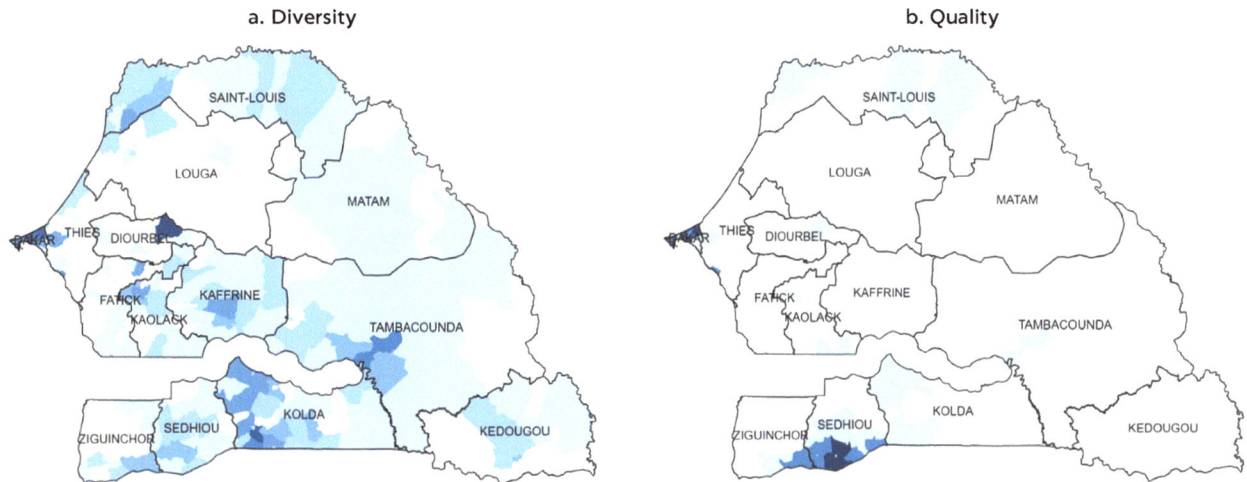

a. Diversity

b. Quality

Source: Cruz, Dutz, and Rodriguez Castelan 2022.
Note: The darker the color, the higher the diversity or quality.

Box 2.2

Identifying local entrepreneurial ecosystems

To identify ecosystems of a broad sector or value chain, the diversity and quality of agglomerations are evaluated. The diversity and quality of agglomerations can be found using a variety of algorithms, depending on the available data. If firm-level data with the exact geographic location of firms (such as census data) are available, Duranton and Overman's (2005) algorithm can be applied. Alternatively, one can also consider many of the new machine-learning techniques that are being developed to identify clusters in a particular economic activity or firms with different potential. If access only to aggregates is available, then measures of local autocorrelation can be used, such as Moran's I (Anselin 1995; Felkner and Townsend 2011). Last, if panel data are available, the measures of quality can be richer, based on firm dynamics such as growth, entry, and exit (see Grover Goswami, Medvedev, and Olafsen 2019).

With these different techniques, diversity is searched for by looking for statistically significant agglomerations of subnational regions with a *high density of establishments within each subsector* in the value chain. The subsectors for which a subnational region is part of an agglomeration are then counted. Subsectors at the 4-digit level should be considered, if possible, but less detailed levels may be used in the

absence of such data. The indicator can then be sorted into three broader measures of diversity: no agglomerations, agglomerations in one subsector, and agglomerations in more than one subsector.

Quality is then searched for. As with diversity, the indicator of quality first looks for agglomerations in measures of *business dynamism*, for example, firms with more than 20 employees and young firms (0–4 years), and measures of the *potential for additional growth*, that is, formal firms and firms where the manager has tertiary education, or actual growth if panel data are available. The indicator of quality then could count the number of quality measures for which a subnational region is part of an agglomeration. The indicator is sorted into three broader measures: no quality agglomerations, agglomerations in one quality indicator, and agglomerations in more than one quality indicator.

The potential for each ecosystem is then defined by the combination of diversity and quality. Many classifications can be constructed by combining these two aspects. For example, the 3×3 broad indicators of diversity and quality can be combined into a typology with nine categories to identify regions with agglomerations in highly diverse industries and with high-quality firms within a value chain (see table 2.1).

TABLE 2.1 Agglomeration types

DIVERSITY INDICATORS	QUALITY INDICATORS		
	AGGLOMERATIONS IN MORE THAN ONE QUALITY INDICATOR	AGGLOMERATION IN ONE QUALITY INDICATOR	NO AGGLOMERATIONS IN QUALITY
Agglomerations in more than one subsector	Multisector and multiquality	Multisector and monoquality	Multisector
Agglomerations in one subsector	Monosector and multiquality	Monosector and monoquality	Monosector

Source: Based on Cruz, Torres, and Tran 2020.

Diversity and quality can then be combined in different ways to determine the potential for each local ecosystem. Combining indicators allows regions with agglomerations in a high diversity of industries and with high-quality firms within a sector or value chain to be identified. Although many classifications are possible, not all combinations may exist in the data[3] and some teams may want to work with more-aggregated classifications. Often, teams can focus on six categories as shown in table 2.1. In this example, cases with no diversity agglomerations are not discussed because an ecosystem effectively does not exist there.

The methodology also allows three aggregate types of ecosystems to be defined: high-potential, maturing, and incipient ecosystems. In addition to the granular classifications illustrated in table 2.1, it can be useful to work with these aggregated groups. *High-potential ecosystems* exhibit agglomerations in *more than one* quality indicator and agglomerations in at least one subsector (that is, the diversity indicator) within the value chain. *Maturing ecosystems* exhibit agglomerations in *one* quality indicator and at least one subsector. Last, *incipient ecosystems* exhibit agglomerations in more than one subsector but *no* quality agglomerations.

The results of the ecosystem classification should be validated by investigating how key firm outputs correlate across ecosystem types. Importantly, indicators chosen to determine the type of ecosystem cannot be chosen as correlates to validate the results. Otherwise, the validation would follow by definition. For example, to illustrate the differences across the high-potential, maturing, and incipient ecosystems in Senegal, table 2.2 shows how two proxies for productivity (average sales per worker and per plant) differ by sector. These results seem to validate the ecosystem classification, given that productivity tends to increase with the potential of the ecosystem. Notably, these productivity proxies were not used to classify the ecosystems.

The ecosystems within each strategic sector can then be analyzed by first examining the geographic distribution of agglomerations. The example from Senegal shows that in agribusiness, diversity is spatially agglomerated across different regions (map 2.2). Casamance (the region in the south including the states of Sédhiou, Ziguinchor, and Kolda) is a diverse agribusiness region, with high densities of businesses in several subsectors. This region is also characterized by spatial agglomerations of high-quality firms. Casamance and Dakar are two entrepreneurial ecosystems in agribusiness in Senegal with high potential based on the agglomeration of multisector and multiquality features. This exercise can be used to capture the initial conditions for the local ecosystem, under the

TABLE 2.2 Sales per worker and sales per plant in high-potential, maturing, and incipient ecosystems in Senegal

million 2016 CFA francs

SECTOR	AVERAGE SALES PER WORKER			AVERAGE SALES PER PLANT		
	HIGH-POTENTIAL ECOSYSTEMS	MATURING ECOSYSTEMS	INCIPIENT ECOSYSTEMS	HIGH-POTENTIAL ECOSYSTEMS	MATURING ECOSYSTEMS	INCIPIENT ECOSYSTEMS
Agribusiness	16.58	3.38	2.12	68.41	12.88	4.21
Tourism	11.52	3.33	2.31	35.42	5.18	4.66
Manufacturing[a]	23.33	2.74	4.57	57.77	5.15	8.37
Retail	29.30	14.26	7.91	36.71	16.17	9.15
Services[b]	14.11	5.37	3.11	55.25	9.73	6.57

Source: Cruz, Dutz, and Rodriguez Castelan 2022.
a. Manufacturing other than food processing.
b. Services other than retail and tourism.

MAP 2.2

Agribusiness ecosystems in Senegal

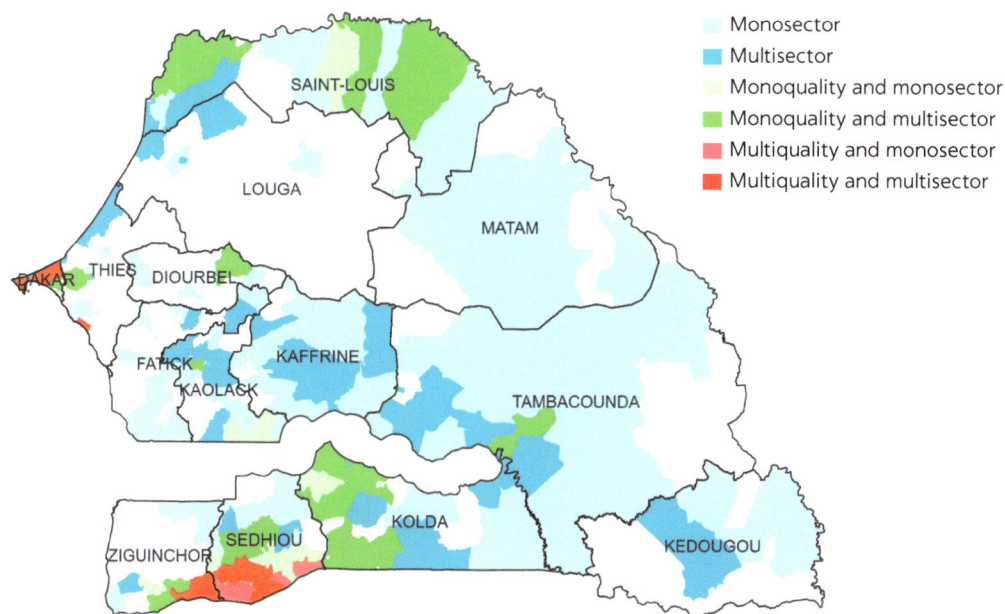

Source: Cruz, Dutz, and Rodriguez Castelan 2022.

assumption that these agglomerations are surrounded by relatively better conditions for the ecosystem pillars, which vary significantly across sectors and regions. (See box 2.3.)

Regions and sectors upon which to focus policy can be identified from the analysis, setting the stage for further analysis and data collection, as needed. The analysis identifies sectors and regions with high growth potential that policy makers may want to focus on. Importantly, policy makers could consider supporting the development of high-potential ecosystems first because they tend to grow more. Therefore, policies that support their development may have more impact on business growth, job creation, and potential spillovers across regions. The analysis can also assist in narrowing the scope for further in-depth data collection, as needed, based on the areas of focus.

Digital entrepreneurial ecosystems

Digital entrepreneurial ecosystems tend to be concentrated in metropolitan areas. As an example, map B2.3.1 shows that Romania's digital ecosystems are concentrated across the Bucharest and Ilfov regions (in dark blue) and show both quality and diversity agglomerations. However, this does not mean that digital firms are not present in other regions. Rather, these two regions show the main potential for growth, following from the high diversity of subsectors and firm performance. Other digital agglomerations exist around Constanta. However, this area does not show the same density of qualitative factors, making Constanta a maturing ecosystem.

For each strategic sector, the analysis can then characterize the found agglomerations by examining their correlations with the main firm indicators.

Table B2.3.1 provides an example, showing the main characteristics of the local digital ecosystems in Romania. This analysis serves to both validate the results of the ecosystem classification and better illustrate their local characteristics. High-potential ecosystems (Bucharest-Ilfov, for example) are the ones with the highest quality, despite agglomerations in other regions. These high-potential ecosystems have the highest share of high-growth firms (35 percent of all such firms in the ecosystem), combined with highly productive businesses (82 percent).[a] Further, these high-potential digital ecosystems do not have the highest concentration of firms but do have a large share of young and large firms. Conversely, in the mature ecosystems, labor and firm productivity are not the highest, but these ecosystems have an important share of high-growth firms.

MAP B2.3.1

Digital ecosystems in Romania

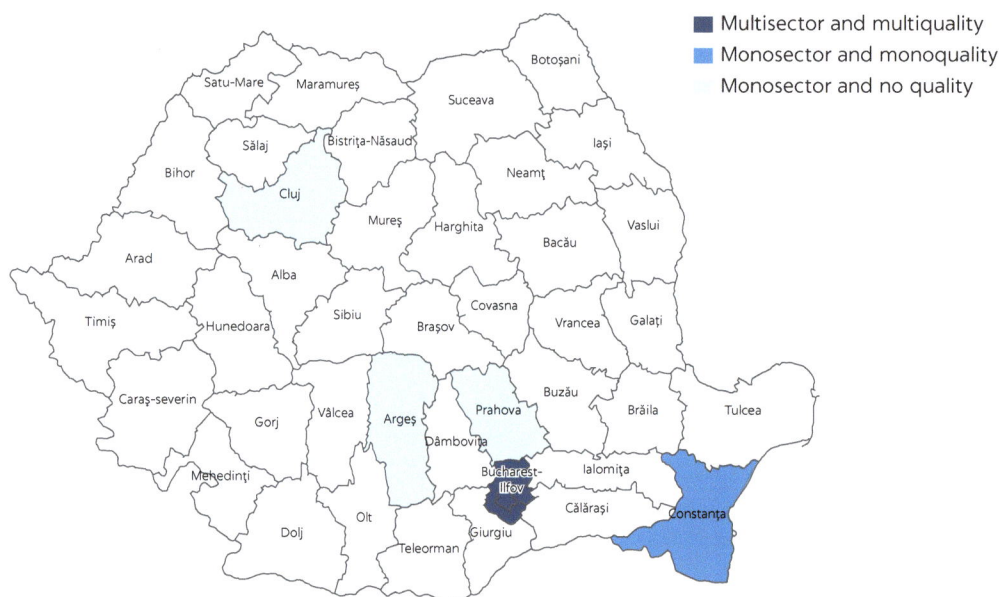

Source: Cruz et al. 2021.

continued

Box 2.3, *continued*

TABLE B2.3.1 **Digital ecosystem indicators in Romania**
percent

TYPE	TOTAL FIRMS		YOUNG FIRMS		LARGE FIRMS		HGF OECD
Multisector and multiquality		10		70		76	35
Multisector and monoquality		0		0		0	0
Monosector and monoquality		5		8		3	29
Multisector and no quality		0		0		0	0
Monosector and no quality		9		15		15	15
No agglomeration and monoquality		14		4		4	11
No agglomeration and no quality		62		4		2	11

TYPE	WORKERS		TURNOVER		HIGHLY PRODUCTIVE BUSINESSES	
Multisector and multiquality		81		89		82
Multisector and monoquality		0		0		0
Monosector and monoquality		3		2		5
Multisector and no quality		0		0		0
Monosector and no quality		12		7		9
No agglomeration and monoquality		3		1		2
No agglomeration and no quality		2		1		2

Source: Cruz et al. 2021.
Note: Young firms = firms less than five years old. Large firms = firms in the 95th percentile of number of employees. HGF (high-growth firms) OECD = firms meeting OECD-Eurostat definition: "All enterprises with average annualized growth greater than 20 percent per annum, over a three-year period, and with 10 or more employees at the beginning of the observation period." For highly productive businesses, productivity is proxied using sales per worker, and the cutoff is set at the 95th percentile of the size distribution. OECD = Organisation for Economic Co-operation and Development.

a. Because this analysis should also validate the ecosystem classification, productivity indicators and high-growth firms were not used to determine whether an ecosystem is high potential, maturing, or incipient.

Conclusions about the required policies for each ecosystem type can also be drawn based on the results. Policies that target a certain geographic area or sector can be tailored to the type of ecosystem. For instance, a high-potential ecosystem would require a different set of measures than a maturing ecosystem. In the Romania example, the high-potential digital ecosystems in Bucharest-Ilfov would benefit from increasing the density of these activities, given that concentration in the digital sector is common. Further, promoting diversity there would generate more knowledge spillovers, and hence more innovation. In the maturing ecosystem of Constanta, although diversity measures would be useful, measures fostering the performance of its firms would be especially beneficial, given the lower quality.

2.3 ENTREPRENEURSHIP CHARACTERISTICS AND PERFORMANCE ACROSS SUBNATIONAL ECOSYSTEMS

This section of the module assesses the subnational outputs, entrepreneurship pillars, and main obstacles faced by firms as well as the demand for policies. The analysis first discusses the entrepreneurship outputs and input pillars across regions, using the cross-country methodology but applying it at the subnational level. It then discusses obstacles faced by firms, combining data on perceived obstacles with factual information. Then, it delves into the policies that firms demand. Last, the section concludes with a summary of policy implications based on these results.

Teams should analyze both perceived and factual obstacles faced by firms. The analysis combines perceived obstacles (what firms report as their main obstacle) with factual information (the local conditions firms actually face). This combination is important to provide clarity on key issues, but also to consider the perception of entrepreneurs, which is relevant for policy dialogue and for understanding their decision-making processes. For example, a perceived lack of market access may actually be the result of a lack of capabilities to produce a more competitive product. In the example of electricity access, the share of firms reporting it as a major constraint can be compared with objective data on the share of firms with access, the number of power outages, and similar information. The main obstacles for analysis can typically include, but are not limited to, (1) access to physical capital, infrastructure, and digital technology; (2) access to human capital; (3) access to markets; (4) the regulatory environment; and (5) access to finance.

To further gauge the importance of perceived obstacles, it is also useful to look at the associations between different constraints and firm growth. Figure 2.1

FIGURE 2.1

Association between largest perceived obstacles and firm growth in Kenya

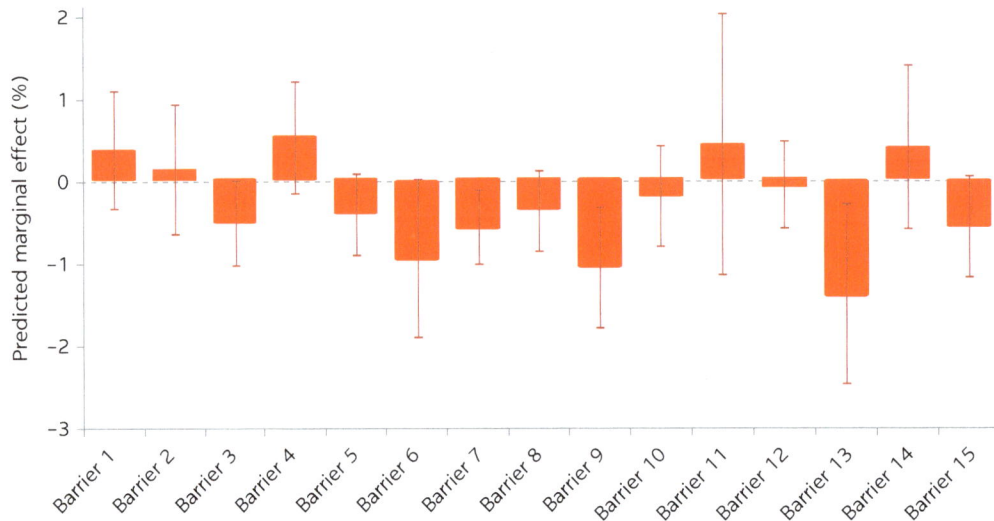

Source: Cruz and Hernandez Uriz 2022; results based on KNBS 2017.
Note: Barriers are as follows: 1: raw material shortage; 2: power interruption; 3: electricity inaccessibility; 4: poor water access; 5: lack of space; 6: lack of skill; 7: lack of markets; 8: local competition; 9: foreign competition; 10: credit collateral shortages; 11: authority interference; 12: licenses; 13: taxes; 14: other government regulations; 15: poor security. Marginal effects based on an ordinary least squares analysis controlling for sector, formal status, county, age groups, and number of workers at the starting year. Vertical lines show 95 percent confidence intervals.

provides an example of this analysis for Kenya. Here, the perceived obstacles related to access to electricity, lack of skills, lack of markets, foreign competition, and taxes (barriers 3, 6, 7, 9, and 13) are negatively and significantly associated with business growth as measured by jobs, even when controlling for sector, formal status, county, age groups, and the number of workers at the starting year. The results suggest that, for an important entrepreneurship outcome such as scale-up, the perceived barriers are indeed associated with performance. Importantly for local policy makers, another similar analysis also shows that there is no significant difference across sectors of the likelihood of these significant obstacles being reported in Kenya. These are just examples of descriptive information that can be extracted from the firm-level data.

The demand for different policies by firms, across different regions, can be analyzed using survey data. Firms' demand for policies will typically, but not necessarily, be in line with their main perceived obstacles. Knowing firms' policy suggestions can help the team better understand firms' constraints, improve the policy dialogue, and design better policies with adequate take-up. This knowledge can also help with refining and prioritizing existing policy options by providing more granular information at times. For example, infrastructure may be a known issue, but firms may report that improving access to electricity is a higher priority than water. Similarly, improving access to public procurement may be the most desired policy among the various options for dealing with a lack of access to markets. Yet, it is important to validate these results with complementary factual analysis identifying the key contribution of these factors.

2.4 DEEP DIVE INTO A LOCAL ECOSYSTEM

Having identified important ecosystems, teams can collect additional targeted data to provide deeper insights into one or a few selected ecosystems. To this end, teams can use surveys within the sector or region of most interest, depending on the findings of the previous analysis. For example, in Romania (box 2.3), there was a demand for delving deeper into digital and tech start-ups. One option is to use a start-up survey, as discussed in section 3.4 of module 3. The analysis should then begin with a description of firm characteristics in the ecosystem of interest (for example, digital and tech start-ups). It should proceed with a detailed analysis of founder and management characteristics. As in the cross-country analysis, within-ecosystem analysis along the output dimensions (scale-up and innovation) and ecosystem pillars should also be conducted. This analysis can therefore complement the broader cross-country work by providing much more targeted information for important ecosystems within a country. It is also important that this section of the analysis discuss the perceived obstacles for firms within the ecosystem of interest. Last, with appropriate data, a connectedness analysis can be done, as described in section 3.5 of module 3.

NOTES

1. The figures and tables presented in this module are illustrative examples extracted from the pilots implemented in Senegal (Cruz, Dutz, and Rodriguez Castelan [2022], describing a methodology developed by Cruz, Torres, and Tran [2020]) and Romania (Cruz et al. 2021). For further details about the results, please consult the references.
2. The OECD-Eurostat definition of high-growth firms is, "All enterprises with average annualized growth greater than 20% per annum, over a three-year period, and with ten or more employees at the beginning of the observation period. Growth is thus measured by the number of employees and by turnover" (OECD 2010, 16).
3. For example, it is possible (and likely) that none of the multisector agglomerations have zero quality agglomerations.

REFERENCES

Anselin, L. 1995. "Local Indicators of Spatial Association—LISA." *Geographical Analysis* 27 (2): 93–115.

Cruz, Marcio, Mark Andrew Dutz, and Carlos Rodriguez Castelan. 2022. *Digital Senegal for Inclusive Growth: Technological Transformation for Better and More Jobs.* International Development in Focus. Washington, DC: World Bank. http://documents.worldbank.org /curated/en/380191643961292189/Digital-Senegal-for-Inclusive-Growth-Technological -Transformation-for-Better-and-More-Jobs.

Cruz, Marcio, and Zenaida Hernandez Uriz. 2022. *Entrepreneurship Ecosystems and MSMEs in Kenya.* Washington, DC: World Bank. https://doi.org/10.1596/38230.

Cruz, Marcio, Natasha Kapil, Pablo Andres Astudillo Estevez, Christopher David Haley, Zoe Cordelia Lu, and Pelin Arslan. 2021. *Starting Up Romania: Entrepreneurship Ecosystem Diagnostic.* Washington, DC: World Bank. http://documents.worldbank.org/curated /en/099920106072238493/P174325083a5cc0eb090350dcde4c6a32df.

Cruz, Marcio, Jesica Torres, and Trang Tran. 2020. "Entrepreneurship Ecosystems in Senegal: Challenges and Opportunities of Digital Technologies." Manuscript, World Bank, Washington, DC.

Duranton, Gilles, and Henry G. Overman. 2005. "Testing for Localization Using Micro-Geographic Data." *Review of Economic Studies* 72 (4): 1077–106. https://doi.org/10.1111/0034 -6527.00362.

Felkner, J. S., and R. M. Townsend. 2011. "The Geographic Concentration of Enterprise in Developing Countries." *Quarterly Journal of Economics* 126 (4): 2005–61.

Grover Goswami, A., D. Medvedev, and E. Olafsen. 2019. *High-Growth Firms: Facts, Fiction, and Policy Options for Emerging Economies.* Washington, DC: World Bank.

Karlsson, Charlie, Jonna Rickardsson, and Joakim Wincent. 2021. "Diversity, Innovation and Entrepreneurship: Where Are We and Where Should We Go in Future Studies?" *Small Business Economics* 56 (2): 759–72. https://doi.org/10.1007/s11187-019-00267-1.

KNBS (Kenya National Bureau of Statistics). 2017. "2016 MSME Basic Report." https://www .knbs.or.ke/download/2016-msme-basic-report/.

OECD (Organisation for Economic Co-operation and Development). 2010. *High-Growth Enterprises: What Governments Can Do to Make a Difference.* OECD Studies on SMEs and Entrepreneurship. Paris: OECD Publishing. https://doi.org/10.1787/9789264048782-en.

Digital Entrepreneurship and Tech Start-ups

3.1 INTRODUCTION

Digital entrepreneurship is characterized by knowledge intensity, creative destruction, and the intense use of data to create value. It tends to be different from traditional entrepreneurship because of the characteristics of the underlying digital technologies and associated business models they follow (Nambisan 2017; von Briel, Davidsson, and Recker 2018). Digital entrepreneurship is more likely to use platform-based or data-driven business models that need to scale up and build network effects (Sussan and Acs 2017).

This module aims to address the following questions:

- What are the dynamics and maturity of digital entrepreneurship in the country?
- What are the key constraints faced by digital entrepreneurs?
- What are the most relevant networks of connectedness for digital start-ups?

A sample structure for this module is provided in box 3.1.[1]

Box 3.1

Digital entrepreneurship and tech start-ups assessment: Proposed structure

A. Digital entrepreneurship pathway (cross-country comparison)

B. Digital entrepreneurial ecosystem: Local landscape
   1. Potential agglomerations of digital entrepreneurship
   2. Digital entrepreneurship output (entry, scale up, exit, innovation)
   3. Ecosystem pillars assessment (start-up survey)

a. Supply-side factors: Physical capital, human capital, and knowledge capital

b. Demand-side factors: Firm capabilities, incentives to invest and accumulate, and entrepreneurial characteristics

c. Barriers to accumulation: Access to finance, regulations, social capital, and culture

C. Connectedness analysis

D. Strengths and challenges for digital entrepreneurship (summary of key findings)

3.2 DEFINITION OF DIGITAL ENTREPRENEURSHIP

The increasing importance of the digital economy has led to disproportionate demand for diagnostics with a focus on digital entrepreneurship and technology-driven start-ups. Policy makers in developing countries put increasing hopes on digital entrepreneurship's high growth potential and transformative power for the wider economy. Although technological leapfrogging may be possible in some areas, developing and supporting a digital entrepreneurial ecosystem requires a thorough analysis of a country's conditions—including structural factors, policies, human and institutional capacity, and financing constraints—and the characteristics of digital entrepreneurship (see also Friederici, Wahome, and Graham 2020). This module aims to provide practical guidance on how to carry out diagnostics focusing on digital entrepreneurship and tech start-ups. Table 3.1 provides an overview of the key elements that define digital entrepreneurship.

Digital entrepreneurs use new business models and technologies with unique characteristics that underpin their transformative power and potential for innovation-driven growth (Brynjolfsson and McAfee 2011). Understanding the underlying fundamentals that differentiate digital business models from traditional ones is essential to identifying the best ways to support them. In particular, these fundamentals relate to economies of scale, network effects, and economies of scope that are driven by the role of data:

- *Economies of scale.* Given the low cost of data storage, computation, and transmission, digital firms are able to scale up their businesses at close to zero marginal costs. For example, a Software as a Service provider may offer the same product to another customer with only marginal increases in fixed and variable costs.
- *Network effects.* Many digital solutions are characterized by the fact that their utility to users increases with the number of people using them. For example, a social networking platform is more attractive to users the more people that are registered. This feature leads to strong advantages for digital companies that have already established extensive network effects, for example, social networking platforms (Evans and Schmalensee 2013; Still et al. 2017).
- *Role of data and economies of scope.* Digital firms are more likely to operate in multiple product markets and amass large amounts of data that are valuable

TABLE 3.1 **Definition of digital entrepreneurship**

KEY ELEMENTS	DETAILS
Risky endeavor, high probability of failure	Digital entrepreneurs develop or use new digital technologies or business models or apply existing ones to a new context (such as a different sector or country). The success of the endeavor is, therefore, inherently uncertain and requires different support mechanisms than other newly established businesses.
Fast growth and scalability due to scope economies via network effects	Digital entrepreneurs intend to grow their businesses into larger enterprises and do not merely set up an organization for self-employment. They aim to scale up the business and expand its market share quickly, including leveraging new digital business models and network effects. (Note: The definition does not exclude the start-up arms of larger and established offline enterprises or conglomerates that are present in many developing countries. Being part of a larger corporation, these start-up units have an intrinsic market access advantage, but their growth potential may be limited by prematurely focusing on serving only the parent company.)
Development or use of novel digital technologies and data at the core of the enterprise	Digital technologies are an integral part of a start-up's service or product offerings. Moreover, digital entrepreneurship is usually at the forefront of using new digital technologies and associated business models, including big data analytics, artificial intelligence, blockchain, or the Internet of Things.

Sources: Based on Nambisan 2017; OECD 2019; Sussan and Acs 2017; von Briel, Davidsson, and Recker 2018.

resources for the improvement and expansion of their digital products and services. Data from one product market may also be beneficial for entering adjacent markets—allowing digital businesses to use economies of scope (Hein et al. 2020; Rochet and Tirole 2003; Thomas, Autio, and Gann 2014). In the context of digital platforms, this is often referred to as "platform envelopment," where a dominant platform can leverage its existing user base from its primary market to enter a new market (see, for example, Bourreau and de Streel 2019). For example, an e-commerce platform can use merchants' transaction data to determine creditworthiness for financial technology (fintech) products. More and more e-commerce platforms have multiple functions and operate in various product markets, including fintech, logistics tech, and foodtech, amplifying their network effects in multisided markets.

- *Scale without mass.* Economies of scale and cross-border flows of data enable digital firms to expand into new markets without needing to establish a physical presence (Ocampo 2019). This leads to a tendency for digital entrepreneurship to face more internationalized competition early on.

However, although these underlying characteristics create unique opportunities, they also cause an inherent risk of market distortion or raise data protection concerns that need to be accounted for. Firms that scale up their business models quickly, capitalize on network effects, and derive economies of scope by reusing data in adjacent sectors or products can become dominant players in markets; that is, they exhibit "winner takes most" tendencies (Crémer, de Montjoye, and Schweitzer 2019; Sturgeon 2021). Although this may result in low marginal costs for consumers, it also creates barriers to entry for new businesses and leads to concentration of market power. Meanwhile, traditional competition policy frameworks are challenged by such dynamics; for example, the definition of markets is complicated by firms that cross-subsidize between product markets or offer nominally free or even negative-price services. Moreover, economies of scope may also pose new data privacy concerns when data from one business function is used for another one without users even realizing it. Therefore, policy makers need to consider such effects on competition and data protection from the outset when supporting digital entrepreneurship to ensure well-functioning markets and consumer trust. Another risk is related to data sharing and reuse, especially by small and medium enterprises in lower-income countries. Although some advanced economies have already set up data exchange platforms or data space to increase the movement of data across government agencies, firms, industries, or even boundaries to create value, this remains an untapped opportunity in most developing economies.

3.3 DIGITAL ENTREPRENEURSHIP PATHWAYS

An assessment of digital entrepreneurship needs to consider countries' different digital entrepreneurship pathways, which are influenced by the endowed factors and the policy environment. The success of digital entrepreneurs is affected by factors that enable digital technologies and new business models to be created, to be adopted, to reach scale, and that allow businesses to engage in equitable competition. Although the conditions that digital entrepreneurs need to succeed (such as market size, the regulatory framework, and access to finance) are not necessarily unique, distinct features apply specifically to digital entrepreneurship. Moreover, although traditional entrepreneurship-support instruments such as incubators, accelerators, or innovation hubs are important for digital entrepreneurship, they are not sufficient to generate a thriving digital entrepreneurial ecosystem. Crucial conditions that affect countries' digital entrepreneurship pathways include the following:

- *Digital market size (demand factor)*. Given the network effects and economies of scope, market size (for example, population and income level) matters. The number of digital businesses in a country is strongly associated with the size of the economy, as measured by the GDP or the population (see Zhu et al. 2022). These factors determine whether there is a critical mass of demand for digital solutions, including from traditional "offline" industries.

- *Availability of financing (allocation effectiveness)*. Digital entrepreneurs find it more difficult than traditional entrepreneurs to access finance such as loans because their mostly intangible assets (for example, software) leave them with little collateral. Moreover, digital start-ups need to grow faster than traditional start-ups to trigger network effects and outpace the more international and fiercer competition they face due to concentration in digital markets and scale without mass. The success of a digital entrepreneurial ecosystem therefore depends on the availability of risk financing, such as venture capital, for early-stage entrepreneurs (Cavallo et al. 2019; Lerner and Nanda 2020). In addition, success also depends on the type of venture capital that is available; corporate venture capital by "big tech" and their potential competition-distorting mergers and acquisitions ("killer acquisitions") may have negative effects on digital entrepreneurship.

- *Conduciveness of the regulatory environment to the digital economy*. Digital entrepreneurship requires digital market regulations that encourage the adoption of digital business models (for example, e-transaction laws), support them to reach scale (for example, industry data policies), and allow them to engage in equitable competition and build trust for digital uptake among consumers (for example, online consumer and supplier protection and antitrust 2.0). General regulations that support entrepreneurship—like those that promote the ease of starting a business—are necessary for digital entrepreneurs but not sufficient to encourage the emergence of digital solutions firms. Another critical issue stems from the lack of clarity on how existing ("offline") regulation applies to the digital setting. Many existing laws (for example, laws on contracts, payments, and intellectual property rights) apply to the digital economy even though they are not specifically tailored to it. This leads to uncertainties about how the rules will be interpreted by regulators and courts and may especially encourage small entrepreneurs to be cautious in implementing new innovations for fear of liability and reputational damage. Incumbent and large firms have the necessary resources and expertise to invest in a better understanding of the law and to fight potential lawsuits. To level the playing field, more proactive guidance on how existing rules apply to digital cases may help digital entrepreneurs.

- *Digital infrastructure, digital payments, and digital skills*. Digital pathways have traditionally been affected by other preconditions of the digital economy, including the scope of the human capital endowment, such as digital and deep-tech skills, as well as the availability and affordability of physical digital infrastructure, digital payment solutions, and digital government services (such as digital ID). Although these are not the focus of this toolkit, they play a role in assessing the likely pathway of digital entrepreneurship in a country.

After gaining an understanding of a country's digital business landscape compared with those of regional or global peers (see box 3.2) and combining it with a country's preconditions, a project team can hypothesize a possible digital entrepreneurship pathway. Broadly speaking, there are three types of countries that share common characteristics for their pathways to digital entrepreneurship development, mainly defined by market size and digital policies. This toolkit supports the notion that not every country needs to create a Silicon Valley of globally leading tech firms to derive value from digital entrepreneurship. Rather, it aims to highlight the potential of different digital entrepreneurship pathways for supporting the economy. Small countries with limited market size may find it to be more beneficial to embrace the advantages of international and regional networks for spillovers of knowledge and technology and greater access to "smart" capital and markets. Some other countries may lack the conditions to create deep-tech digital solutions firms but could reap large gains from digitally enabled entrepreneurship, for example, promoting fintech solutions for traditional ("offline") industries or adopting e-commerce to help exporting firms (Audretsch et al. 2022). Policy priorities for digital entrepreneurship need to be set in acknowledgment of the different pathways.

Countries may encounter three broad types of digital pathways:

- *Type 1: Large economies* such as Brazil, the Russian Federation, India, and China (the so-called BRICs countries), but especially India and China, have sufficient domestic market size to allow digital start-ups to develop minimum viable products and reach scale. However, as described above, population size is not sufficient but needs to be considered in conjunction with income level and digitalization propensity (for example, availability of digital skills, digital infrastructure, and level of digital adoption within traditional industries). Although large economies are not constrained by a lack of market size, digital entrepreneurship will not automatically emerge given that an enabling digital regulatory and business framework (for example, e-commerce laws, public data sharing) is critical. Moreover, the case of Japan (box 3.3) shows that even large economies with sound foundations for digital entrepreneurship risk falling behind if, for example, they lack international vision and face other contestability distortions (such as a strong role for conglomerates).
- *Type 2: Small, open economies with proactive policies* compensate for their limited market size and serve as the regional "centers of gravity" of digitalization, for example, by applying supportive regulations on cross-border flows of data, money, and talent. This group includes countries such as Estonia (box 3.4), Israel, New Zealand, and Singapore (see Mulas et al. 2021). The countries in this group often serve as regional digital hubs given their integration into international digital markets. Digital start-ups in these small, open economies tend to pursue business strategies with a focus on regional or international markets early on because their home markets are often not large enough for them to reach scale. In addition to their openness, supporting factors for countries in this group are cultural proximity to neighboring countries' markets (for example, language, overlap in popular culture, political history) as well as the language skills of start-up owners.
- *Type 3: Small, closed economies* are in a difficult position from which to grow their digital entrepreneurial ecosystems (box 3.5). Their market size is insufficient to support digital start-ups that exclusively focus on domestic customers, and their closed economies deter digital founders from expanding abroad

Box 3.2

The World Bank Digital Business Database: A tool for assessing the landscape of investment-ready digital solutions firms and deal flows

The World Bank has assembled a global digital business database to support countries in assessing their digital business landscape, especially vis-à-vis peer countries. This Digital Business Database of the Finance, Competitiveness, and Innovation (FCI)

Global Practice contains firm-level data on digital solutions firms from three proprietary data sources (CB Insights, PitchBook, and Briter Bridges) with more sources being added as annual updates become available, for example, Crunchbase and

FIGURE B3.2.1

Examples of using the FCI Digital Business Database for analyses in the Latin America and the Caribbean region

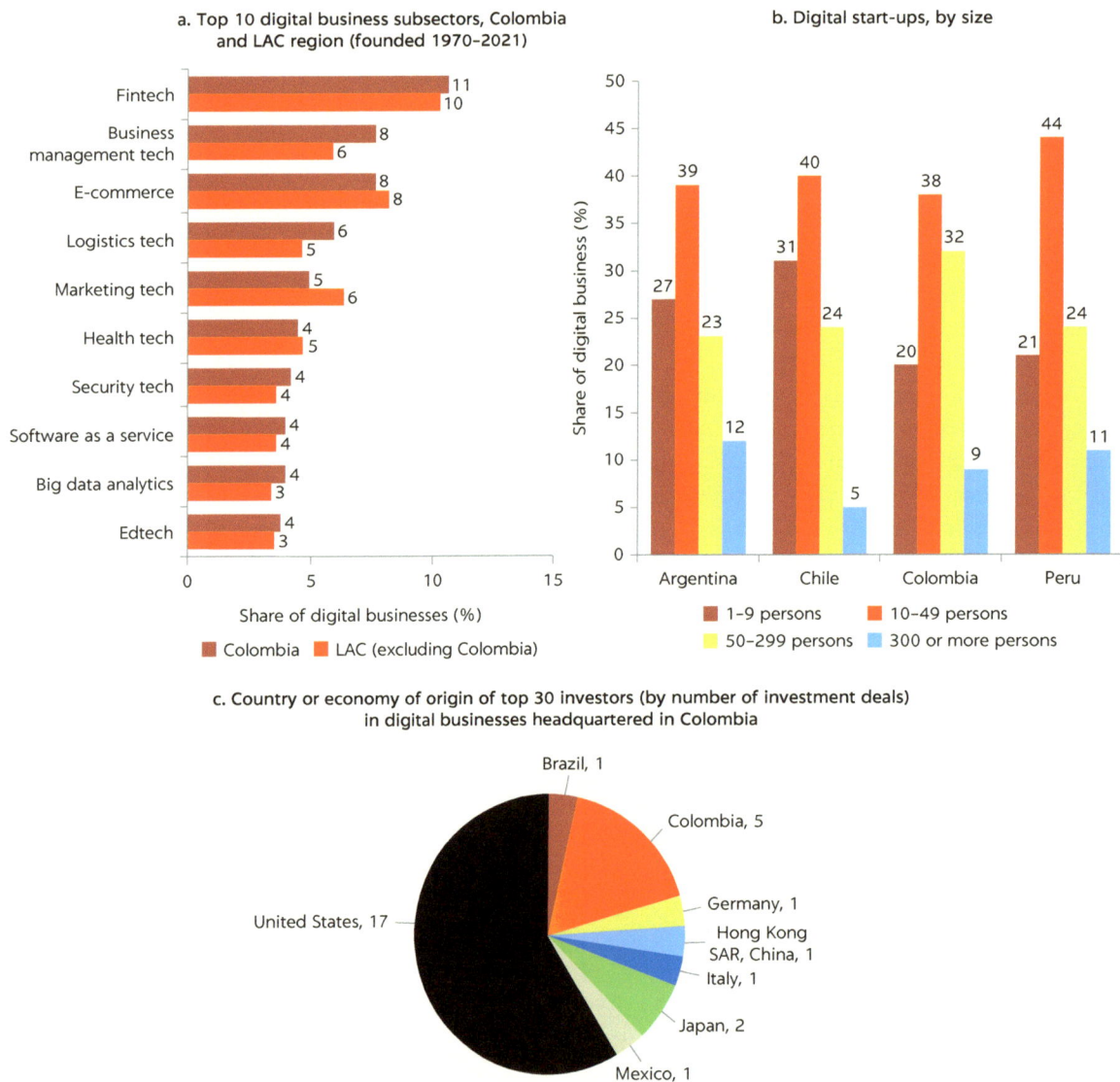

a. Top 10 digital business subsectors, Colombia and LAC region (founded 1970–2021)

b. Digital start-ups, by size

c. Country or economy of origin of top 30 investors (by number of investment deals) in digital businesses headquartered in Colombia

Source: Illustrative analysis for the digital economy for LAC—digital business assessment using the World Bank Finance, Competitiveness, and Innovation (FCI) Global Practice Digital Business Database (focus on Colombia and LAC). See also Zhu et al. 2022.
Note: LAC = Latin America and the Caribbean.

continued

Box 3.2, *continued*

Thomson Reuters. The data were collected using a variety of techniques, including web scraping and the gathering of firm information from entrepreneurship networks and venture capital (VC) or other investment deals. The data providers specialize in collecting information on tech start-ups and digitalized firms that may be attractive for risk capital investors because of certain innovative elements in their business models or core product offerings. The database includes about 200,000 digital businesses in 190 countries across all World Bank regions, harmonized and categorized in 44 digital subsectors such as fintech, e-commerce, health tech, and software as a service. The database contains information about each firm's characteristics (such as name and address, company description, and sector), location (headquarters and operating country), digital business model variables (such as digital platform or data-driven business), and funding performance as of 2020 (for example, total funding amount, name of investors, exit dates, and type), and the database is scheduled to be updated every other year as a global public good.

The World Bank's Finance, Competitiveness, and Innovation (FCI) Global Practice Digital Business Database provides a unique resource with which to analyze various aspects of digital entrepreneurship, including numbers of digital businesses over time, patterns of digital subsectors in countries, as well as investor and merger and acquisition activities. These benchmarkable data analyses can be compiled in a standardized country-level PowerPoint within one to two weeks. The database can be used to identify which digital subsectors receive how much funding by investors in a particular country relative to its peers. This allows the identification of market-ready technologies and business models, assessments of the maturity of a country's digital business landscape—for example, by considering the types of exits (such as mergers and acquisitions or initial public offerings) or age of firms— and the identification of trends in the contestability landscape (such as the extent of big tech players acquiring digital businesses in their own or adjacent subsectors). Illustrative examples of standard country analyses from the database are provided in figure B3.2.1.

Box 3.3

Type 1: Large economies—Nigeria and Japan

With a population of more than 200 million, Nigeria, a lower-middle-income country, has substantial market size. Although the true number of digital businesses that operate in the country is difficult to estimate, the Finance, Competitiveness, and Innovation Digital Business Database (Zhu et al. 2022) provides evidence of more than 600 investment-ready digital businesses as of 2020— making it an overperforming country relative to its GDP and population. Nigeria's digital businesses tend to operate in financial, social media, business services, and education industries with increasingly innovative business models that fill service gaps in the country (Zottel et al. 2021). The large domestic market with entrepreneurial hubs, especially in Lagos, but also in Abuja and Port Harcourt,

has originated several successful digital businesses, such as the e-commerce companies Jumia and Konga, which since have expanded into further markets. Nigeria has established itself as a regional hub with a growing number of digital companies that are headquartered there while also operating in other countries in the region (mainly West Africa, but also in the Arab Republic of Egypt, Kenya, and South Africa). Nigeria is overperforming despite several gaps in its regulatory framework for digital entrepreneurship. For example, as of 2020 the country has no law governing intermediary liability or electronic transactions— an important legal aspect to clarify the responsibility of e-commerce platforms. However, in recent years there have been legislative efforts that have

continued

Box 3.3, *continued*

helped fill regulatory gaps, including in the areas of cybercrime, cybersecurity, taxation of digital services, and data protection.

Meanwhile, Japan provides an example of the risk that a country with a large market size, advanced technology companies, and high levels of digital skills and infrastructure can still fall behind in digital entrepreneurship. Japan has been a leader in technology and innovation for many decades, with a large share of its GDP being spent on research and development (Mulas et al. 2021). However, the digital business gap indicator shows that the country is underperforming relative to its GDP and population. Japan's start-up ecosystem is relatively small for a country of its size and has produced limited results (Mulas et al. 2021). Among a multitude of reasons, it stands out that

Japan's start-up ecosystem has fewer international connections, as illustrated by the fact that all of the top 20 investors (by number of deals) in digital businesses headquartered in Japan are from Japan (World Bank 2022). This limits the transfer of knowledge and the building of international business networks and market expansions. Moreover, a large share of venture capital financing is provided by corporate venture capital—reflecting the strong role of conglomerates in Japan—which risks reducing market contestability through the premature acquisition of start-ups before they reach full potential. In Tokyo, for example, more than 60 percent of funding rounds involve corporate venture capital—substantially higher than in Seoul, Beijing, or the United States (Mulas et al. 2021).

Box 3.4

Type 2: Small, open economies—Estonia

Since the launch of its E-Estonia initiative, the small Baltic country with a population of 1.3 million has established itself as a global front-runner in digitalization. E-Estonia builds on multiple pillars, including the digitalization of nearly all government services, advanced e-identity (e-ID) solutions, and data interoperability and security. For example, Estonians can use their unique e-ID to pay bills, vote online, sign contracts, shop, and access their health information. Through the E-Residency program, these benefits are extended to noncitizens who can easily register companies in Estonia solely through digital means. As of 2021, more than 80,000 foreigners had become e-Residents and started more than 16,000 companies (e-Estonia, n.d.). About 800 non-EU founders have received a visa or temporary residency through Estonia's start-up visa program, which focuses on technology-based, innovative, and scalable businesses that are reviewed by a selection committee comprising members of Estonia's start-up community (Startup Estonia, n.d.).

Estonia's case study shows how a small country can leverage digital opportunities with progressive, decisive, and proactive policy measures that embrace international integration. Despite its small size, Estonia has supported the rise of many digital start-ups, especially in software as a service and fintech (OECD 2020). Estonian founders and cofounders have started seven companies that have become unicorns, that is, start-ups valued at US$1 billion: Bolt, ID.me, Pipedrive, Playtech, Skype, Transferwise (now Wise), and Zego (Startup Estonia 2021). Although many factors have contributed to the success of digital start-ups in Estonia, an important one has been the government's focus on creating X-Road, a secure and interoperable infrastructure for the exchange of public and private data. X-Road is the information backbone of Estonia's digital society and has contributed to increasing trust in digital transactions and the sharing of data.

Box 3.5

Type 3: Small, closed economies—Benin

Although not a unique case study, Benin illustrates some of the challenges that small, closed economies face with regard to digital entrepreneurship. The economy of the lower-middle-income country with a population of 12 million people relies heavily on agriculture and informal trade with neighboring Nigeria (20 percent of GDP) (World Bank 2023). Despite progress in the expansion of digital infrastructure (for example, access to submarine cable networks) and updating of digital regulations, the country faces multiple challenges, including a lack of digital skills and low rates of mobile broadband internet penetration (World Bank 2021). Although Benin has a growing number of entrepreneurship support organizations (such as incubators and accelerators), it has had only limited success in producing digital start-ups. However, the rapid adoption of digital payment services in the country is expected to provide solid ground for digitalization of services in the coming years. Other factors that will provide benefits in advancing the digitalization process are the recent creation of a public platform providing all basic public administrative services to the population and the creation of a digital commerce platform for agriculture and handicraft value chains. For Benin, the opportunity provided by its digital and digitally enabled entrepreneurs is to tap into regional markets and networks. The West African Economic and Monetary Union and the Economic Community of West African States will be key for Benin's digital business growth.

because of regulatory hurdles and discourage outsiders from entering the local market. Because market size and many factor endowments for the digital ecosystem are inflexible in the short run, it may be more beneficial for policy makers to focus on leveraging regional investor networks and intermediary organizations to introduce fit-for-purpose digital solutions to serve the analog economy and stimulate digital uptake and productivity. The demonstration effects can inspire younger generations, hopefully leading to indigenous digital solutions businesses.

3.4 THE START-UP SURVEY INSTRUMENT

A more comprehensive perspective on the digital and high-tech ecosystem can be obtained through a start-up survey, which can also serve as the basis for the connectedness analysis to be discussed next. The World Bank has developed a start-up survey instrument, which was piloted in Romania (see Cruz et al. 2021), that comprises six sections: basic characteristics of the firm, founder and management characteristics, development stage and funding, access to knowledge and networks, obstacles to entrepreneurship, and performance and prospects. The questionnaire for a start-up survey can be found in online appendix C.[2] An example of general analysis using such data for Romania is given in box 3.6. Further, the survey can also be used as a basis for the connectedness analysis described in section 3.5.

The definition of start-ups is controversial and often not rigorous, creating challenges for the survey's target group. *Start-ups* could be simply defined as new firms. This definition captures a widely accepted dimension of start-ups—they are new or young firms—and it facilitates the availability of comparable data across countries and regions. However, it does not convey a qualitative component that is usually present in policy discussions and practitioners, which

Box 3.6

Characterizing start-up founders in Romania

Founders in the high-potential sample are usually better educated than those in the tech start-up sample. Most founders in the tech start-up sample have college and master's degrees, 12.7 percent of them do not have a college degree, and 2.8 percent have a PhD (figure B3.6.1, panel a). Most firm founders in the high-potential sample have college and master's degrees, 16 percent have a PhD, and 1 percent do not have a college degree. Women founders in the high-potential sample usually have higher educational attainment than their male counterparts (figure B3.6.1, panel b). Note that the tech start-up sample uses a sampling frame of national business registry data with firms that are less than five years old in the information and communication technology sector and

tech product manufacturing, whereas the high-potential sample uses a sampling frame from commercial data sources such as PitchBook and CB Insights.

The findings from the pilot in Romania suggest that founders in the high-potential sample are more experienced in the sector and are usually more likely to have experience abroad than those in the tech start-up sample. About 34 percent of firm managers in the tech start-up sample have either worked or studied abroad, mostly in other European countries (figure B3.6.2, panel a). By comparison, 76 percent of founders in the high-potential sample have either worked or studied abroad (figure B3.6.2, panel b), mostly in the United States (69 percent) or in European countries (26 percent). Moreover, firms in the high-potential

FIGURE B3.6.1

Founders' highest degree or level of education

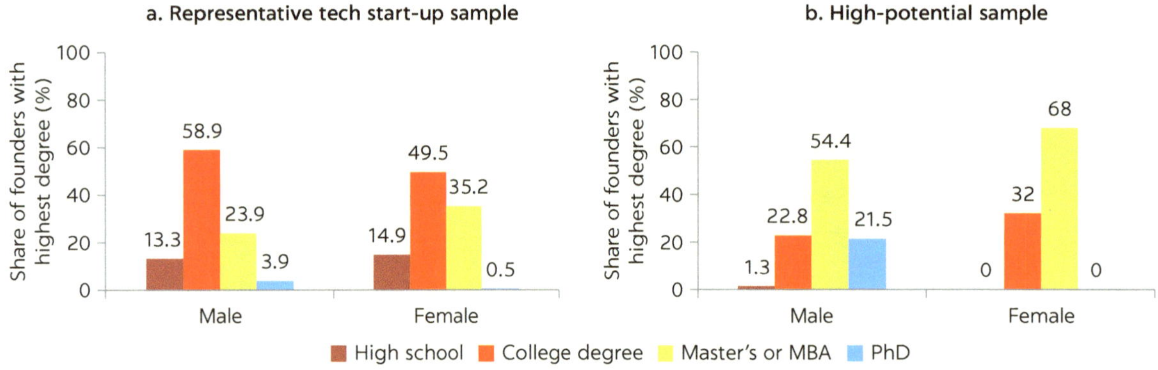

a. Representative tech start-up sample

b. High-potential sample

Legend: High school | College degree | Master's or MBA | PhD

Source: Cruz et al. 2021.
Note: MBA = master of business administration.

FIGURE B3.6.2

Founders' experience abroad

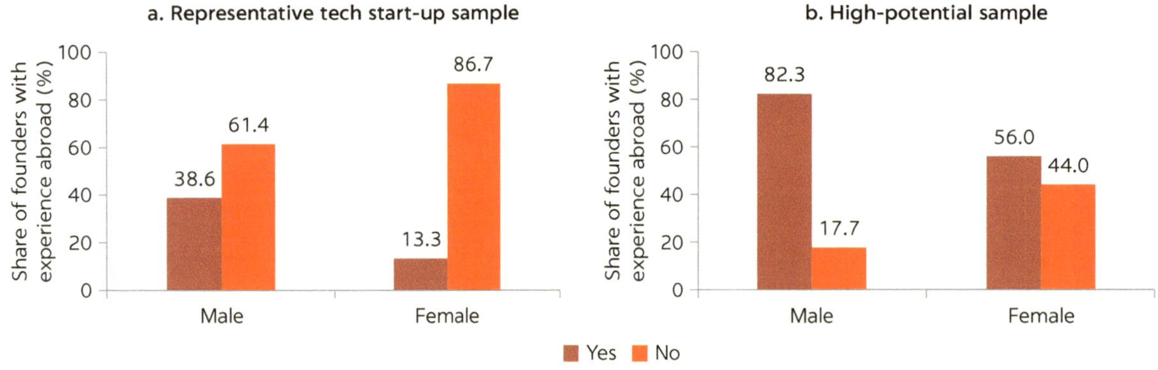

a. Representative tech start-up sample

b. High-potential sample

Legend: Yes | No

Source: Cruz et al. 2021.

continued

Box 3.6, *continued*

sample were more likely to have both founders with previous experience in the same sector and founders with previous experience starting a business. Few of the founders in the tech start-up sample had similar experience. Finally, firms' top managers tend to be their founders: in both samples, 93 percent to 95 percent of the firms report that one of the founders is the top manager of the company.

The two biggest obstacles to entrepreneurship reported by firms in both samples in Romania were business regulations and the lack of an entrepreneurial mindset (see figure B3.6.3). Regulations, which were identified as an issue in every Romanian region, included labor regulations and administrative issues such as permits and taxes.

FIGURE B3.6.3

Main business obstacles faced by tech start-ups

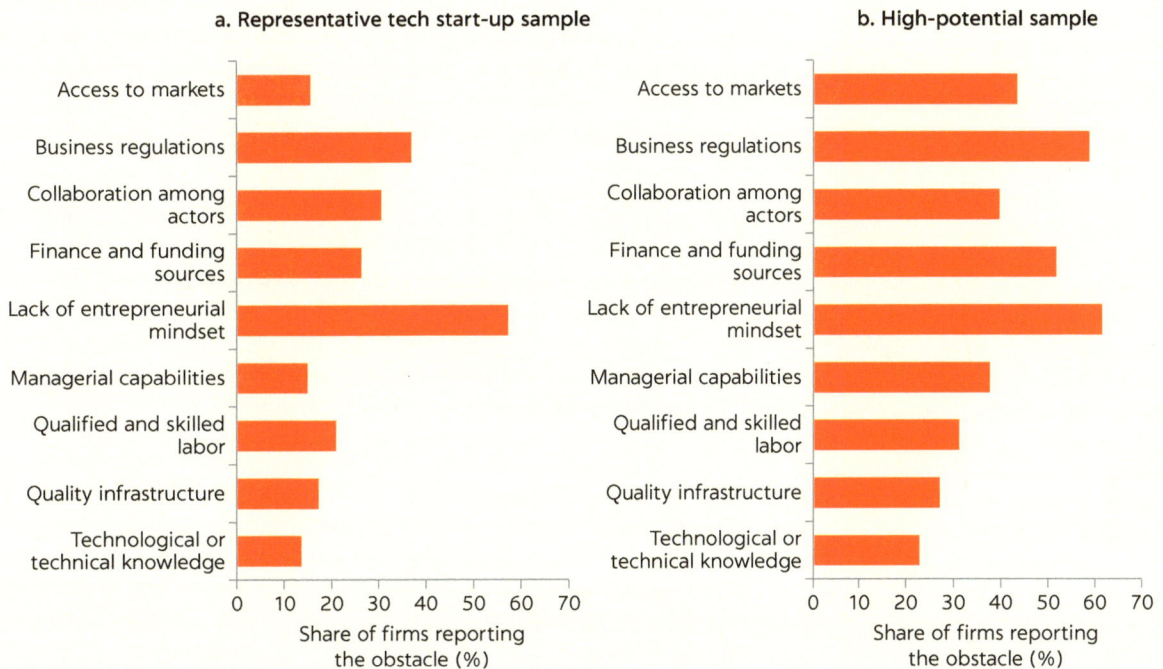

Source: Cruz et al. 2021.

suggests that start-ups are *innovative, technology-based, digital, high-growth,* or *high-potential* firms. Incorporating this qualitative component into empirical work and observing it in the data to find survey respondents is therefore challenging.

To overcome issues stemming from the definition of start-ups, the pilot in Romania used two samples of firms: the "tech start-up" and the "high-potential." The tech start-up sample was based on a representative sample of firms from the establishment census, focused on firms fitting a standard and readily observable definition of a tech start-up, based on age and sector (mostly digital businesses following the sector classification proposed by the US Bureau of Economic Analysis; see Barefoot et al. 2018), especially when access to the national establishment census was available. The high-potential sample was based on venture-capital–backed firms, aiming to capture firms with the qualitative characteristics that are often of interest to policy makers in terms of high-growth aspirations. This population of high-potential start-ups can be considered an aspirational benchmark in the analysis, while the representative sample allows for further understanding the potential bias of venture capital–backed firms. For the sake of comparability for the pilot in Romania, the high-potential sample was merged with the establishment census to keep a consistent sector definition.

The representative tech start-up sample was defined as containing young tech firms, which can be specified in a variety of ways. Depending on the country, different age and sector specifications can be used to determine young tech firms. For example, teams can often refer to a country's start-up laws for a definition. Typically, however, this sample would include firms age five years or less in digital business solutions or high-tech manufacturing sectors.

The high-potential sample can be drawn from proprietary data, such as that provided by CB Insights, PitchBook, and Crunchbase, with the caveat that the data may not be representative. Instead, the firm sample from these data sources tends to perform better than the average tech or high-potential firm given that they usually have already passed the research and development and product testing stage and are investment-ready and are hence being captured by commercial proprietary data sources. The constraints they face are therefore a lower-bound estimate—the overall tech ecosystem can face more, and more severe, constraints, and the average tech firm will not have the capability and resources with which to address them.

3.5 CONNECTEDNESS ANALYSIS

The connectedness of an ecosystem refers to the interdependencies and interactions among its constituting actors. These actors can include founders, universities, incubators, accelerators, mentors, financiers, and others. The links between them can vary substantially by the quantity and quality of their interactions. These links are particularly relevant for knowledge-intense tech or digital start-ups because they measure the knowledge spillover effects.

Human networks are a critical element of entrepreneurial ecosystems and are key to explaining why one ecosystem outperforms another. Networks support the identification of entrepreneurial opportunities, access to finance, access to information, the creation of resources, strategic alliances, and status signaling. Further, spillovers can occur when highly connected entrepreneurial actors can access or transmit ideas and knowledge within networks. Similarly, highly connected entities enhance innovation and learning while facilitating entrepreneurship (Scott, Hughes, and Ribeiro-Soriano 2021). In addition, the social networks of an entrepreneurial ecosystem connect all other elements so entrepreneurs can access the resources needed to create start-ups and ease institutional barriers.

The conceptual importance of connectedness in entrepreneurial ecosystems is supported by significant prior research and theoretical modeling (see, for example, Eesley, Hsu, and Roberts (2014); Kaplan (2012); Porter (1998); van Winden et al. 2014). Previous works that consider connectedness in entrepreneurial ecosystem assessments include the "Global Startup Ecosystem

Report 2018" (Startup Genome 2018), "The Power of Entrepreneur Networks" (Endeavor Insight 2014), and the 2018 World Bank–GEN "Ecosystem Connections Mapping" (GEN 2018).

Hence, understanding and measuring connectedness is important because it can serve as a proxy for social capital and can improve policy making at various stages. Connectedness is a form of social capital, which in the conceptual framework is linked to policies and institutions through the implicit interactions between the policy layer and ecosystem pillars. Further, understanding the locations and structure of ecosystem connections allows policy makers to better structure their programs. In particular, information about connectedness allows policy targeting based on high-potential cluster areas rather than simply on geography, which can maximize intervention gains. Further, it allows policies to target actors with the richest connections, thereby maximizing the effects across the ecosystem, or those with the least connections to help them escape underperformance. Finally, measuring the quantity and quality of connectedness will give policy makers a better sense of their ecosystem's status, thereby improving monitoring and comparisons over time and against other ecosystems.

The connectedness analysis therefore has three broad goals. The first is to identify key players in the ecosystem, that is, those that can have the most influence if targeted by interventions. The second is to identify clusters[3] in the ecosystem and analyze their structure, coverage, and trends. This analysis can include their investments, knowledge sharing, and so on. The third is to understand the links between actors (firms, support institutions, and policy makers) and identify the interdependencies between seemingly isolated local ecosystems and the policy instruments that can help strengthen these links.

The analysis should be supported by standard network measures. Network measures can allow the amount and quality of connections between relevant actors of the entrepreneurial ecosystem to be measured. Hence, they can be a suggestive indicator of how information and knowledge flow across the ecosystem's entrepreneurs, workers, and institutions. For example, there might be significant heterogeneity in the quality and roles of different institutions and entrepreneurs in the ecosystem. The possible network measures to be considered are introduced in box 3.7.

The network measures can be constructed using a variety of data sources, including the start-up survey. Official data sources, such as the firm census or household surveys, can be used when available. If no official data are available, teams can consider implementing a custom survey, such as the start-up survey described in section 3.4, to identify the key players and their interactions. Finally, alternative data collection, such as web scraping or proprietary data,[4] can also be used, especially using investment deal flows to identify investor centrality. However, alternative data may not be representative because there could be selection bias.

The following questions, among others, can potentially be answered through network analysis:

- *Spillover effects.* What is the impact of a program on nontargeted firms and institutions connected to the program's direct beneficiaries via networks? Note that answering this question requires adequate data on the program beneficiaries as well as connectedness data on these beneficiaries.

Box 3.7

Network measures

In a network analysis, the nodes of the network represent the individual entities (start-ups, investors, accelerators or incubators, mentors, universities, and so on), and the edges (links) represent the relationships that exist between them. Calculating the centralities of the nodes allows the most important players in the ecosystem to be identified. In this context, three measures can be calculated:

- *Degree centrality* measures the number of other nodes within the ecosystem to which each node is directly connected.

- *Eigenvector centrality* measures the importance of a given node based on the importance of the other nodes that are associated with it.
- *Modularity* measures the strength of the connections between the nodes and detects the communities (groups, clusters) that exist in the network.

- *Ecosystem connectedness.* How connected is the ecosystem (both internally and externally), and what are the general patterns or trends in an ecosystem's connectedness? Note that benchmarking the level of connectedness requires data on other ecosystems.
- *Connectedness and geographic distribution.* Check for patterns in groups geographically. Do certain clusters or entity types dominate?
- *Central actors, intermediaries, and relationships.* Which is the most central actor or set of actors in the ecosystem? Which entities are bridging the most connections (especially for intermediaries)? Are there entities that are crucial go-betweens for the ecosystem clusters or subnetworks? Do certain entities have information or diverse network advantages over other similar entities?
- *The impact of connectedness on outcomes.* Do better-connected firms or intermediary institutions perform better than less-connected counterparts?

Connectedness analysis can also be used for ecosystem network visualization. Creating interactive visualizations of the relationships between the key actors in the ecosystem, taking institutions and firms as nodes and their relationships as connections, is helpful to prioritizing resources. These visualizations not only provide a more concrete understanding of how different ecosystem actors interact, but also enables the identification of actors (core and peripheral) and network properties (such as clustering) based on connectedness. An example of a network visualization is provided in box 3.8.

Universities, accelerators, and incubators will typically be among an ecosystem's top players because of their key positions within networks. These entities are critical to facilitating connections and knowledge exchange. They usually hold more information, which they can instantly connect and spread throughout the wider network. However, this does not necessarily mean that universities are actively promoting entrepreneurship. Rather, as a result of their size and importance, they are crucial producers of human and social capital. Studies (Mulas and Gastelu-Iturri 2016; Mulas et al. 2021) show that most successful start-ups are usually associated (through alumni networks) with the country's key universities (figure B3.8.1, panel b). Similarly, successful

Box 3.8

An example of connectedness analysis in Romania

The Romania Startup Survey for the high-potential sample included several questions to identify the relations between entities that are part of the entrepreneurial ecosystem and their respective locations. The start-ups were asked where their founders had studied, who their investors were or who had offered them financial support, which accelerators or incubators had supported them, who the founders' mentors were, and so on. Using the answers, a network of relations was built, and a network analysis was performed.

The network analysis shows that three universities are the top players in Romania's entrepreneurial ecosystems. Polytechnic University of Bucharest, the University of Bucharest, and Babes-Bolyai University are the most connected entities and the ones with the most important connections within the ecosystem (figure B3.8.1, panel a).

Accelerators and incubators are the second-most important group of players in the ecosystem, while only one central entity provides funding. The most relevant accelerators and incubators in the ecosystem are InnovX, Techcelerator, and StepFWD. GapMinder VC was the only key player in the ecosystem that provided funding. This is unusual and may reflect the relatively undeveloped state of venture capital in Romania and the widespread use of personal savings rather than debt or equity.

The data reinforce the importance of the Bucharest-Ilfov ecosystem for Romania, with few enablers outside of the main hubs. Including a geographic dimension in the network (by geo-localizing all the entities) shows that the predominant connections are between Bucharest, Cluj-Napoca, Iasi, Timisoara, and Constanta (figure B3.8.2). These local ecosystems rely on each other, mostly for human capital, social capital, and finance. However, most of the local start-ups relate to Bucharest's universities, accelerators, and funders. The data also show that firms rely little on their local ecosystems, except in Bucharest and Cluj-Napoca. Therefore, improving the Bucharest ecosystem could generate important externalities for other ecosystems in the country, regardless of their economic activity. Additionally, more attention on all other regions is needed to build links and strengthen ecosystem support structures across Romania.

FIGURE B3.8.1

Romanian entrepreneurial network and clusters

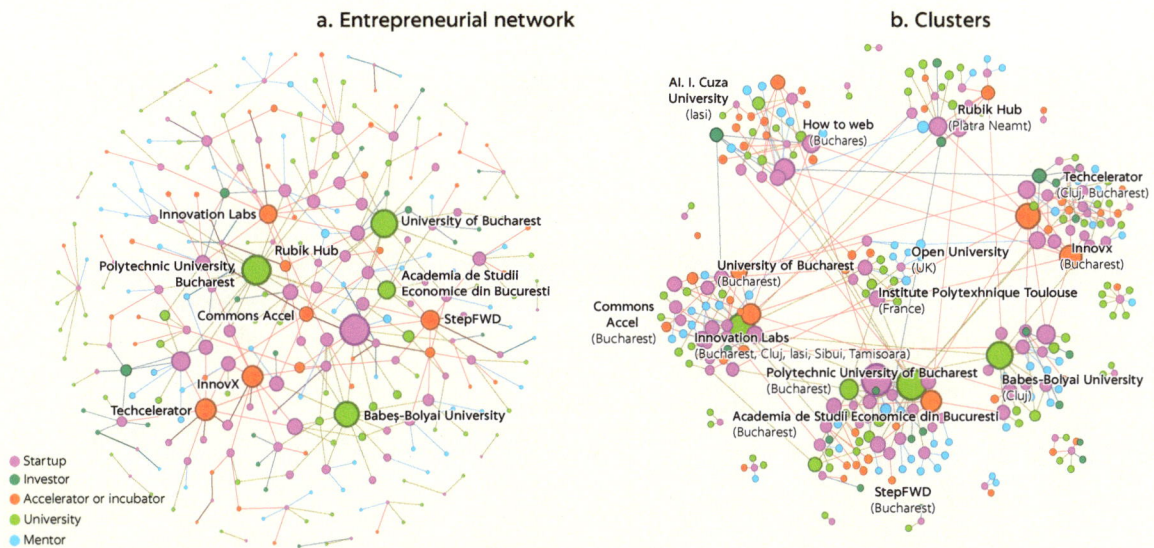

a. Entrepreneurial network

b. Clusters

Source: Cruz et al. 2021.
Note: Panel a shows the connectivity of the complete ecosystem. Each circle's size is the centrality, that is, how connected each entity is. Panel b shows the clusters (communities) that form the Romanian start-up ecosystem. Cities in **bold** are mentioned in box 3.8.

continued

Box 3.8, *continued*

Most of the few Romanian start-up international connections are with the United States and the United Kingdom. These connections are usually with foreign universities or investors. However, this connectedness is small in comparison with the domestic connections, given that fewer than 10 percent of total connections are international. These international connections are key to the success of start-ups because this kind of connectedness can improve human and social capital as well as help start-ups achieve a better understanding of larger markets and build trust with international actors.

FIGURE B3.8.2
Local ecosystem connectedness

Source: Cruz et al. 2021.
Note: The links represent connections between entities in the Romanian start-up ecosystem. The thickness of the lines represents the importance of these links (the number of connections between the cities).

start-ups are also commonly associated with international and experienced accelerators, which are also key providers of social capital. Therefore, interventions in such central entities could typically generate positive externalities for the entire national ecosystem.

NOTES

1. The figures and tables presented in this module are illustrative examples extracted from the complementary projects that harmonized the World Bank Digital Business Database (Zhu et al. 2022) and the pilot implemented in Romania (Cruz et al. 2021). For further details about the results, please consult the references.
2. Online appendixes A through F are available at https://openknowledge.worldbank.org /handle/10986/40305.

3. A cluster is defined as a dense network of companies and institutions in a certain geographic sphere.
4. See online appendix F for more details.

REFERENCES

Audretsch, David B., Maksim Belitski, Rosa Caiazza, and Matthias Menter. 2022. "Editorial: Technology Adoption over the Stages of Entrepreneurship." *International Journal of Entrepreneurial Venturing* 14 (4/5): 379–90.

Barefoot, K., D. Curtis, W. Jolliff, J. R. Nicholson, and R. Omohundro. 2018. "Defining and Measuring the Digital Economy." Working paper, US Department of Commerce, Bureau of Economic Analysis, Washington, DC.

Bourreau, Marc, and Alexandre de Streel. 2019. "Digital Conglomerates and EU Competition Policy." Available at SSRN. https://doi.org/10.2139/ssrn.3350512.

Brynjolfsson, Erik, and Andrew McAfee. 2011. *Race against the Machine: How the Digital Revolution Is Accelerating Innovation, Driving Productivity, and Irreversibly Transforming Employment and the Economy.* Lexington, MA: Digital Frontier Press.

Cavallo, Angelo, Antonio Ghezzi, Claudio Dell'Era, and Elena Pellizzoni. 2019. "Fostering Digital Entrepreneurship from Startup to Scaleup: The Role of Venture Capital Funds and Angel Groups." *Technological Forecasting and Social Change* 145 (August): 24–35. https://doi.org/10.1016/j.techfore.2019.04.022.

Crémer, Jacques, Yves-Alexandre de Montjoye, and Heike Schweitzer. 2019. *Competition Policy for the Digital Era.* Brussels: European Commission.

Cruz, Marcio, Natasha Kapil, Pablo Andres Astudillo Estevez, Christopher David Haley, Zoe Cordelia Lu, and Pelin Arslan. 2021. *Starting Up Romania: Entrepreneurship Ecosystem Diagnostic.* Washington, DC: World Bank. http://documents.worldbank.org/curated/en/099920106072238493/P174325083a5cc0eb090350dcde4c6a32df.

e-Estonia. n.d. "Facts & Figures." Accessed March 20, 2023, https://e-estonia.com/facts-and-figures/.

Eesley, C. E., D. H. Hsu, and E. B. Roberts. 2014. "The Contingent Effects of Top Management Teams on Venture Performance: Aligning Founding Team Composition with Innovation Strategy and Commercialization Environment." *Strategic Management Journal* 35: 1798–817.

Endeavor Insight. 2014. "The Power of Entrepreneur Networks: How New York City Became the Role Model for Other Urban Tech Hubs." Endeavor Global, New York. http://www.nyctechmap.com/nycTechReport.pdf.

Evans, David S., and Richard Schmalensee. 2013. "The Antitrust Analysis of Multisided Platform Businesses." Working Paper 18783, National Bureau of Economic Research, Cambridge, MA.

Friederici, Nicolas, Michel Wahome, and Mark Graham. 2020. *Digital Entrepreneurship in Africa: How a Continent Is Escaping Silicon Valley's Long Shadow.* Cambridge, MA, and London, England: MIT Press.

GEN (Global Entrepreneurship Network). 2022. "Ecosystem Connections Mapping." https://www.genglobal.org/research/ecosystem-connections-mapping.

Hein, Andreas, Maximilian Schreieck, Tobias Riasanow, David Soto Setzke, Manuel Wiesche, Markus Böhm, and Helmut Krcmar. 2020. "Digital Platform Ecosystems." *Electronic Markets* 30 (1): 87–98. https://doi.org/10.1007/s12525-019-00377-4.

Kaplan, S. 2012. *The Business Model Innovation Factory: How to Stay Relevant When the World Is Changing.* Hoboken, NJ: Wiley.

Lerner, Josh, and Ramana Nanda. 2020. "Venture Capital's Role in Financing Innovation: What We Know and How Much We Still Need to Learn." Working Paper 20-131, Harvard Business School, Cambridge, MA.

Mulas, Victor, Pablo Astudillo, Takashi Riku, Jamil Wyne, and Xin Zhang. 2021. "Tokyo Start-Up Ecosystem." World Bank, Washington, DC. https://openknowledge.worldbank.org/handle/10986/36462.

Mulas, Victor, and Mikel Gastelu-Iturri. 2016. "New York City: Transforming a City into a Tech Innovation Leader." Working paper, World Bank, Washington, DC. https://doi.org/10.1596/25753.

Nambisan, Satish. 2017. "Digital Entrepreneurship: Toward a Digital Technology Perspective of Entrepreneurship." *Entrepreneurship Theory and Practice* 41 (6): 1029–55. https://doi.org/10.1111/etap.12254.

Ocampo, Andrés Felipe Ramírez. 2019. "Scale without Mass: Permanent Establishments in the Digital Economy." IBDT Actual. https://revista.ibdt.org.br/index.php/RDTIAtual/article/download/1842/1540/5653.

OECD (Organisation for Economic Co-operation and Development). 2019. *The Missing Entrepreneurs 2019: Policies for Inclusive Entrepreneurship.* Paris: OECD Publishing. https://www.oecd-ilibrary.org/industry-and-services/the-missing-entrepreneurs-2019_3ed84801-en.

OECD (Organisation for Economic Co-operation and Development). 2020. *Boosting Social Entrepreneurship and Social Enterprise Development in Estonia: In-Depth Policy Review.* Paris: OECD Publishing. https://doi.org/10.1787/8eab0aff-en.

Porter, M. E. 1998. "Clusters and the New Economics of Competition." *Harvard Business Review* 76 (6): 77–90.

Rochet, Jean-Charles, and Jean Tirole. 2003. "Platform Competition in Two-Sided Markets." *Journal of the European Economic Association* 1 (4): 990–1029. https://doi.org/10.1162/154247603322493212.

Scott, S., M. Hughes, and D. Ribeiro-Soriano. 2021. "Towards a Network-Based View of Effective Entrepreneurial Ecosystems." *Review of Managerial Science* 16: 157–87.

Startup Estonia. n.d. "I Am a Foreign Founder." Accessed March 20, 2023, https://startupestonia.ee/visa/eligibility-foreign-founder.

Startup Estonia. 2021. "Estonia—#1 in Europe in Number of Unicorns per Capita." April 19, 2021. https://startupestonia.ee/blog/estonia-1-in-europe-in-number-of-unicorns-per-capita.

Startup Genome. 2018. "Global Startup Ecosystem Report 2018: Succeeding in the New Era of Technology." https://startupgenome.com/reports/global-startup-ecosystem-report-gser-2018.

Still, K., M. Seppänen, H. Korhonen, K. Valkokari, A. Suominen, and M. Kumpulainen. 2017. "Business Model Innovation of Startups Developing Multisided Digital Platforms." 2017 IEEE 19th Conference on Business Informatics (CBI), Thessaloniki, Greece, 70–75. doi:10.1109/CBI.2017.86.

Sturgeon, Timothy J. 2021. "Upgrading Strategies for the Digital Economy." *Global Strategy Journal* 11 (1): 34–57.

Sussan, Fiona, and Zoltan J. Acs. 2017. "The Digital Entrepreneurial Ecosystem." *Small Business Economics* 49 (1): 55–73. https://doi.org/10.1007/s11187-017-9867-5.

Thomas, Llewellyn D. W., Erkko Autio, and David M. Gann. 2014. "Architectural Leverage: Putting Platforms in Context." *Academy of Management Perspectives* 28 (2): 198–219. https://doi.org/10.5465/amp.2011.0105.

van Winden, W., E. Braun, A. Otgaar, and J. J. Witte. 2014. *Urban Innovation Systems: What Makes Them Tick?* London: Routledge.

von Briel, Frederik, Per Davidsson, and Jan Recker. 2018. "Digital Technologies as External Enablers of New Venture Creation in the IT Hardware Sector." *Entrepreneurship Theory and Practice* 42 (1): 47–69. https://doi.org/10.1177/1042258717732779.

World Bank. 2021. *Évaluation de l'économie numérique Rapport pays Bénin* [Digital Economy Assessment Country Report Benin]. Washington, DC: World Bank. https://thedocs.worldbank.org/en/doc/61714f214ed04bcd6e9623ad0e215897-0400012021/related/Benin-DE4A-Draft-Report-Version-finale-FR.docx.

World Bank. 2022. "Digital Business Indicators." Research & Outlook. World Bank, Washington, DC. https://www.worldbank.org/en/research/brief/digital-business-indicators.

World Bank. 2023. "The World Bank in Benin." World Bank, Washington, DC. https://www
.worldbank.org/en/country/benin/overview.

Zhu, Juni Tingting, Philip Grinsted, Hangyul Song, and Malathi Velamuri. 2022. "A Spiky Digital
Business Landscape: What Can Developing Countries Do?" World Bank, Washington, DC.
https://openknowledge.worldbank.org/entities/publication/8a3c8fdb-00f2-4a85-b2cd
-e0ce7b830db0.

Zottel, Siegfried, Tingting Juni Zhu, Ana Cristina Alonso Soria, and Yoon Keongmin. 2021.
"Regulatory Analysis: Digital Entrepreneurship in Nigeria." World Bank Group, Washington,
DC. https://documents1.worldbank.org/curated/en/099062823151013200/pdf
/P167399088635b0260b2e3061ffffaf10f6.pdf.

2 Mapping

Mapping Public Programs and Intermediary Organizations

4.1 INTRODUCTION

The mapping of public programs and intermediary organizations (IOs) is the second phase of the entrepreneurial ecosystem analysis, resulting in an institutional and policy mix assessment. The mapping of both public programs and IOs seeks to obtain detailed information about support providers' goals, interventions, resources, beneficiary targets, management characteristics, and monitoring and evaluation (M&E) processes. They also gather and analyze data on public expenditure to foster entrepreneurship, who is providing the public expenditure, and what objectives the expenditure is to achieve.

A key difference between these two mappings is the unit of reference. Public program mapping pertains to programs of government institutions at different levels but does not usually analyze the institution (for example, the ministry) itself; one program can have multiple instruments and, hence, analyses can also be done at the instrument level (for example, start-up grant as an instrument is different from start-up business training). The targets for the IO mapping are organizations that support entrepreneurship themselves, mostly beyond public agencies, without typically analyzing their individual instruments separately. For example, IOs can include incubators, accelerators, networking and information platforms, industry associations, and others. After the two separate mappings, this exercise then compares, relates, validates, and summarizes the analysis on programs, instruments, and IOs, with the final objective of identifying potential gaps, overlaps, and the consistency of the policy mix compared with the main policy objectives and potential market failures identified in modules 1 and 2. A sample structure for the mapping exercise is given in box 4.1.[1]

Countries typically provide support mechanisms across different agencies that foster entrepreneurship, without having an overall picture of their main objectives and budget allocations. This issue is exacerbated by the fact that entrepreneurship activities involve multidimensional areas, leading to a number of initiatives across different agencies and ministries. In many developing

Box 4.1

Mapping public programs and intermediary organizations: Proposed structure

A. Introduction
B. Methodology
C. Public programs
    1. Services provided by objective and ecosystem factor
    2. Intervention mechanisms
    3. Resources available, sources of funding, and expenditure categories
    4. Beneficiary characteristics
    5. Management characteristics
    6. Monitoring and evaluation
    7. Summary

D. Intermediary organizations
    1. Characteristics of institutions supporting entrepreneurship
    2. Services provided by objective and ecosystem factor

    3. Intervention mechanisms
    4. Resources available, sources of funding, and expenditure categories
    5. Beneficiary characteristics
    6. Management characteristics
    7. Monitoring and evaluation
    8. Summary

E. Summary of the policy mix
    1. Complementarities between public programs and intermediary organizations
    2. Supply of services versus perceived barriers and demand
    3. Association between programs' characteristics and services provided

F. Validation exercise

countries, particularly low-income countries, the lack of clarity also extends to programs supported by donors. The same applies to IOs (public or private).

Clarity on the entrepreneurship initiatives and resources already available is critical because often the most valuable policy advice concerns evaluating, improving, and optimizing existing initiatives. Surprisingly, many governments, including those in middle- and high-income countries, lack clarity on all existing initiatives and resources allocated to support businesses, let alone having any rigorous mechanism for monitoring and evaluating those programs. Without this perspective, the effort to provide evidence-driven policy recommendations is constrained. This lack of information leads to a higher probability of gaps, redundancy, and lack of consistency between policies and the development goals of the ecosystem. Further, these issues do not only occur at the national level, but also across different spheres of government (for example, national versus subnational levels).

Mapping is also important for gaining an understanding of whether interventions are connected and whether there is support at different stages of entrepreneurship, or whether support is concentrated around particular phases. An approach that considers the entire firm life cycle is important because the economic impact of entrepreneurship only occurs when ventures scale up, but there is often disproportionate focus on just the start-up process. Figure 4.1 lists policy instruments to be considered in the mapping exercise and illustrates their relation to the firm life cycle.

FIGURE 4.1

Mapping of policy instruments across the business cycle

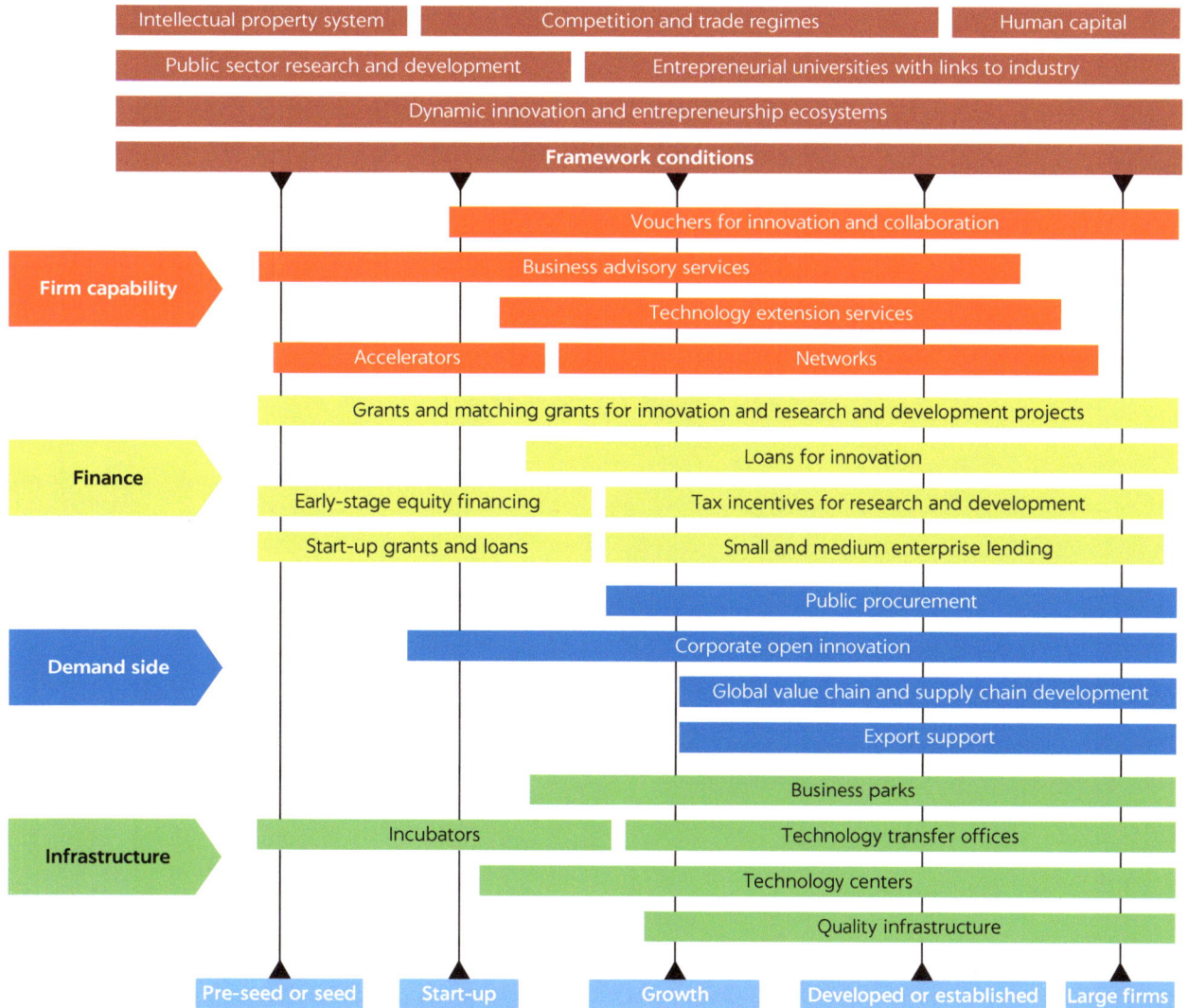

Source: Cirera et al. 2020.

This module aims to address the following questions:

- What resources, main objectives, and characteristics of public programs are currently targeted to supporting entrepreneurship?
- What institutional characteristics (size, managers, organizational structure) and support opportunities for IOs are currently available in the ecosystem?
- Are the current programs targeting innovative and high-growth entrepreneurship?
- Are the public programs following best practices of design, implementation, and governance?
- Is the mix of interventions aiming to support entrepreneurship consistent with the policy objectives, and do the interventions cover the key pillars of the ecosystem?
- Where are the redundant overlaps or gaps, considering the level of development of the entrepreneurial ecosystem?

4.2 MAPPING PUBLIC PROGRAMS

Public policy mapping helps identify existing programs supporting entrepreneurship, analyzes their characteristics, and examines their consistency with development goals. This methodology is based on the World Bank's Public Expenditure Review in Science, Technology, and Innovation, which is a useful resource for teams working on entrepreneurial ecosystems (Correa 2014).[2] The unit of observation for the policy mapping is typically the program or instrument and not the overall implementing institution (for example, a ministry) itself. The mapping identifies the current distribution of public interventions, their coverage of ecosystem pillars and expected outcomes, and their budget structure. Further, the mapping describes these public programs by looking at the characteristics of their beneficiaries and managers as well as their M&E processes. An example of such analysis is provided in section 4.4.

A wide range of policies and variables can be considered in the public policy mapping. Table 4.1 provides an initial list of public policies to be considered, based on the World Bank's innovation policy guide (Cirera et al. 2020). Potential variables that can be used are also discussed in online appendix A.[3] These general lists should then be complemented by desk research and interactions with private sector development specialists who are familiar with the country in question.

The first stage in conducting the public program mapping is to identify the key agencies and public institutions that are leading programs to support businesses. Typically, teams can consider starting with the ministries for economy, industry, trade, enterprise development, innovation, information and communication technology, youth, gender, culture, sports, or agriculture. Other relevant institutions may be agencies for micro, small, and medium enterprises or innovation, enterprise funds for women or youth, national productivity or training centers, securities exchanges, or development authorities. Such institutions can be approached to help with the relevant data collection. This is not an exhaustive list of suggested institutions, and not all of them may be relevant in a country. Further, after identifying institutions, a key challenge can be determining which of their programs are truly related to entrepreneurship. For example, at first glance, many youth-related programs may seem generally relevant. However, a program only focusing on youth employment should be excluded, while one with a component of micro, small, and medium enterprise and entrepreneurship support should be included. An example of the process for identifying key institutions for Kenya is given in online appendix A.[4]

Two main data approaches for the policy mapping exercise can be pursued, each with distinct advantages: (1) administrative data focusing on public expenditure and (2) a survey collecting primary data. Compared with surveys, administrative data provide more complete coverage of existing programs as well as more precise information, especially on budget allocations. Hence, administrative data are typically ideal for assessing existing policy instruments. However, such data may be unavailable or more time consuming to collect, especially in lower-income countries. Surveys, on the other hand, allow information to be collected that would otherwise be unavailable. Institutions involved in entrepreneurship should be targeted as survey respondents. Details on data collection for both approaches can be found in section 4.5.

4.3 MAPPING NONGOVERNMENT INSTITUTIONS AND ORGANIZATIONS SUPPORTING ENTREPRENEURSHIP

The entrepreneurial ecosystem analysis goes beyond public programs to include IOs because nongovernmental actors also play an important role. However, information on IOs is not readily available for many developing countries. Most of these organizations are associated with the supply of physical, human, and knowledge capital, or they focus on lowering the barriers for the allocation and accumulation of these factors. They do so by providing or facilitating access to finance and information, or assist with the implementation of regulations, but they also enhance social capital. Hence, IOs can be analyzed similarly to public programs. In contrast to the public program mapping, however, IOs are typically analyzed as a whole and not through each of their individual instruments. An example of such analysis is given in section 4.4.

The first step in the IO mapping is to identify the wide variety of key institutions that are part of the ecosystem that should then be approached for survey responses. It is important to consider the many different types of possible IOs for this mapping exercise. Table 4.1 provides a nonexhaustive list with examples of IOs supporting entrepreneurship, organized by factor of the ecosystem pillars.[5] In some ecosystems, the list can go well beyond these instruments. The analysis is then typically based on surveys of these IOs.

TABLE 4.1 List of potential institutions to be mapped

ECOSYSTEM PILLAR	FACTOR	ORGANIZATIONS, INSTITUTIONS, ACTORS	DATA SOURCES FOR DESK WORK	PROPOSED DATA COLLECTION INSTRUMENTS TO FILL IN GAPS
A. Supply factors (inputs)	Physical capital and infrastructure	Incubators Tech hubs Spaces for supporting entrepreneurship Investment promotion agencies Networking and information platforms	Websites of government institutions (for example, ministry of science and innovation, ministry of commerce or industry) Reports	Web scraping of incubator or hub websites and directories Proprietary data on incubators and hubs (for example, Crunchbase, PitchBook) Survey to assess institutions' characteristics Web-based surveys such as the WB-GERN Ecosystems Mapping
	Human capital	Universities Educational organizations offering training and courses on entrepreneurship	Websites of government institutions (for example, ministry of education) Reports	Web scraping of university websites and directories Survey to assess institutions' characteristics Web-based surveys such as the WB-GERN Ecosystems Mapping
	Knowledge capital	Research consortiums Organizations focused on extension services Labs Specialized agencies supporting entrepreneurship Specialized agencies supporting technology adoption	Websites of government institutions (for example, ministry of science and innovation) Reports on innovation	Data from government open data websites (and use optical character recognition automated tools to aggregate data if needed) Survey to assess institutions' characteristics Web-based surveys such as the WB-GERN Ecosystems Mapping

continued

TABLE 4.1, *continued*

ECOSYSTEM PILLAR	FACTOR	ORGANIZATIONS, INSTITUTIONS, ACTORS	DATA SOURCES FOR DESK WORK	PROPOSED DATA COLLECTION INSTRUMENTS TO FILL IN GAPS
B. Demand (firms)	Market access	Export promotion agencies Supplier development programs	Websites of government institutions (for example, ministry of science and innovation, ministry of commerce or industry) Reports	Web scraping of incubator or hub websites and directories Proprietary data on incubators and hubs (for example, Crunchbase, PitchBook) Survey to assess institutions' characteristics Web-based surveys such as the WB-GERN Ecosystems Mapping
C. Accumulation and allocation barriers	Access to finance	Development banks Accelerators Angel investors Venture capital Networking and information platforms	Website of government institutions (for example, ministry of industry or commerce) Reports	Web scraping of accelerator and investor websites and directories Proprietary data on accelerators and investors (for example, Crunchbase, PitchBook) Survey to assess institutions' characteristics Web-based surveys such as the WB-GERN Ecosystems Mapping
	Regulations	Quality and standards institutions Institutions responsible for patent applications	Websites of government institutions (for example, ministry of science and innovation) Reports on innovation	Data from government open data websites (and use optical character recognition automated tools to aggregate data if needed) Survey to assess institutions' characteristics Web-based surveys such as the WB-GERN Ecosystems Mapping
	Social capital and culture	Industry and cluster associations Chambers of commerce Networking and information platforms	Websites of government institutions (for example, ministry of industry or commerce) Reports	Data from government open data websites (and use optical character recognition automated tools to aggregate data if needed) Web scraping of alternative data sources Survey to assess institutions' characteristics Web-based surveys such as the WB-GERN Ecosystems Mapping

Source: Original table for this publication.
Note: GERN = Global Entrepreneurship Research Network; WB = World Bank.

4.4 EXAMPLES OF PUBLIC PROGRAM AND IO MAPPING

The analyses for the mapping of public programs and IOs can follow similar structures, after characterizing the types of existing IOs. The dimensions of analysis for both public programs and IOs are typically the same and only differ by whether the results refer to one or the other. Hence, similar data can be collected and analyzed in each case. Notably, public program mapping typically refers to programs of government institutions and not to the institutions themselves. For IOs, it is often useful to look at their general type, as shown in figure 4.2, based on the pilot from Kenya. In particular, IOs can be private, public, nongovernmental, or other types of organizations.

Public programs and IOs can be analyzed according to their ultimate and specific objectives focusing on entrepreneurship. First, teams can start with

FIGURE 4.2

General characteristics of intermediary organizations, Kenya

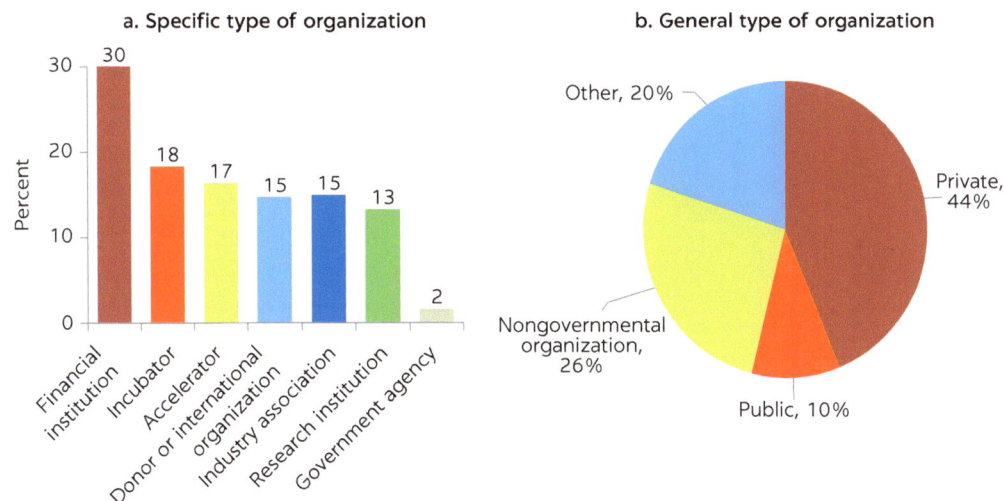

a. Specific type of organization

b. General type of organization

Source: Cruz and Hernandez Uriz 2022.
Note: Panel a is based on 60 observations; panel b is based on 61 observations.

the ultimate objectives, characterized in broad categories, as shown in figure 4.3, panel a, based on the pilot in Romania. Then, the analysis could go deeper, according to more specific and detailed activities, which can yield a different picture (figure 4.3, panel b), as suggested by the results for Romania. This focus on detail is necessary because some "entrepreneurship-related" activities (such as improving access to finance or promoting technology diffusion) are quite broad. Further, some non-entrepreneurship instruments (such as general "digitalization" programs that benefit start-ups) may also benefit entrepreneurs. Detailed activities can also be intermediate routes by which a general, ultimate, objective is achieved. For example, a program might approach the goal of improving competitiveness by improving management practices. These analyses can focus on budget allocations or simply the number of public programs.

Objectives of firm support programs can be grouped into four broad categories, based on their stated ultimate (top-level) objective: (1) entrepreneurship, (2) innovation and competitiveness, (3) digitalization, and (4) research and development (R&D). Although all four categories are directly or indirectly relevant, the rationale for this classification is to better understand the main mechanisms (that is, type of support) by which start-ups and scale-ups might be supported. Objectives categorized under entrepreneurship typically target new or younger firms, whereas programs in innovation and competitiveness are typically more inclusive of all firm sizes and provide support more on the product innovation side. Objectives under digitalization typically provide support for the acquisition of digital equipment and focus more on the process innovation side. Objectives under R&D typically focus on earlier stages of research, development, and innovation. Whereas the innovation and competitiveness category focuses on later stages of product innovation, the R&D category focuses on the earlier stages. However, there is a degree of overlap between the categories, and some programs and IOs have multiple objectives that fit in several categories.

FIGURE 4.3
Entrepreneurship support, by objective

a. Distribution of estimated STI public budget allocation, by top-level objective, 2014-20

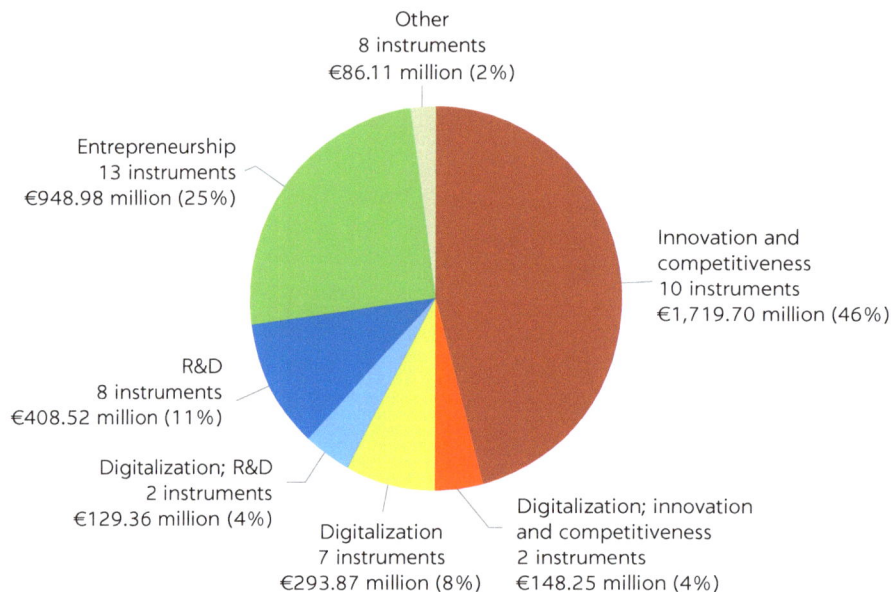

Other
8 instruments
€86.11 million (2%)

Entrepreneurship
13 instruments
€948.98 million (25%)

Innovation and
competitiveness
10 instruments
€1,719.70 million (46%)

R&D
8 instruments
€408.52 million (11%)

Digitalization; R&D
2 instruments
€129.36 million (4%)

Digitalization
7 instruments
€293.87 million (8%)

Digitalization; innovation
and competitiveness
2 instruments
€148.25 million (4%)

b. Public program estimated budgets, by specific objective

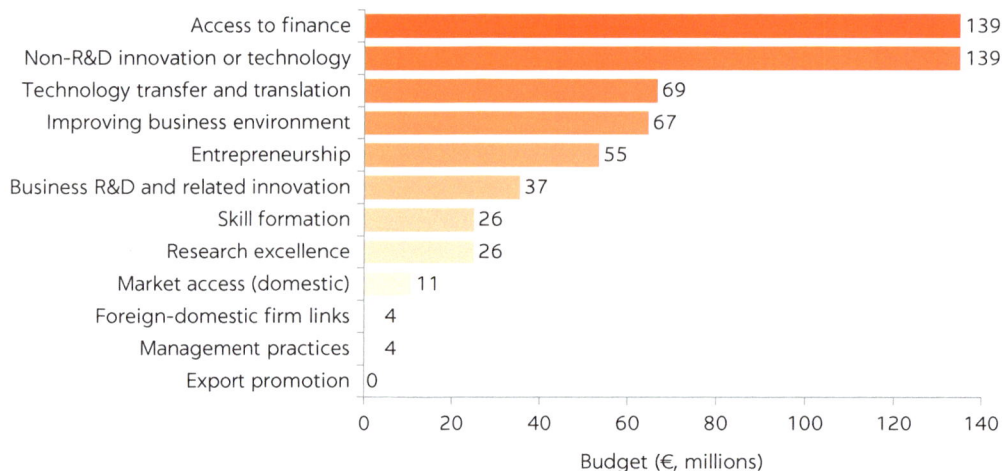

Objective	Budget (€, millions)
Access to finance	139
Non-R&D innovation or technology	139
Technology transfer and translation	69
Improving business environment	67
Entrepreneurship	55
Business R&D and related innovation	37
Skill formation	26
Research excellence	26
Market access (domestic)	11
Foreign-domestic firm links	4
Management practices	4
Export promotion	0

Budget (€, millions)

Source: Cruz et al. 2022.
Note: R&D = research and development; STI = science, technology, and
innovation.

Programs and IOs can also be analyzed by the ecosystem factor they support.
This analysis can be performed by examining simple distributions across the
ecosystem pillars and factors (similar to figure 4.3, panel b), or by relating them
to firm characteristics (such as targeted age and sector). Figure 4.4 shows a
sample heatmap of the support for ecosystem factors by sector, based on the pilot
for Kenya. It reveals that not all factors receive the same support, thereby helping
identify gaps. Note that the regulatory environment can often appear but with
little to no funding because it would not typically be targeted by entrepreneurship
instruments in some countries.

FIGURE 4.4

Entrepreneurship support budget, by ecosystem factor

Pillar	Ecosystem factors	No sector	Agriculture	Manufacturing	Other services
Supply	Physical capital				
	Human capital				
	Knowledge capital				
Barriers	Access to finance				
	Regulations				
	Culture or network				
Demand	Market access				
	Managerial training				
	Change of mindset				

Source: Cruz and Hernandez Uriz 2022.
Note: The darker color suggests the allocation of more resources toward the factor or sector.

Entrepreneurship support can differ according to the intervention mechanisms used, which is crucial for the mapping exercise. Support can come in a variety of ways, such as through grants, networking opportunities, technology parks, incubators, accelerators, education, various services, procurement instruments, tax incentives, loan subsidies, credit guarantees, equity finance, vouchers, and more. Analyzing the types of support is crucial. Therefore, looking at detailed mechanism breakdowns, as well as broader ones, such as financial versus nonfinancial support, can be instructive. Mechanism analysis can include examining program and budget distributions according to instrument type (similar to figure 4.3, panel b), or by relating them to program objectives, as shown in figure 4.5. The mechanisms can also be broken down by type of program or IO. For example, privately run IOs may be more likely to provide financial support than nongovernmental organizations.

Analyzing the funding sources for public programs and IOs is important, and the sources will naturally differ. Public programs are often funded by the central government, provincial governments, international donors, the private sector, or other sources, as shown in figure 4.6, panel a. A common form of private funding for public programs can come from the beneficiaries themselves, for example, through matching grants. IOs typically receive some combination of public, private, and international donor funds as well as fees for services provided. Their funding composition also tends to vary by the type of IO, as shown in figure 4.6, panel b.

Analyzing entrepreneurship support by direct beneficiary type and characteristics is also an important step in the mapping exercise. Public entrepreneurship programs and IOs can have different types of direct beneficiaries, such as firms, research institutes, financial institutions, and so on. Hence, it is important to analyze the distribution of the number of and budget allocation for programs and IOs according to type of beneficiary, as in figure 4.7, panel a. Further, supported firms can also vary widely according to the targeted firm size, sector, region, firm age, firm stage (seed, start-up, scale-up, mature), and so on. Hence, the distribution of programs by these characteristics is important to

FIGURE 4.5

FIGURE 4.5

Entrepreneurship programs, by broad type and objective

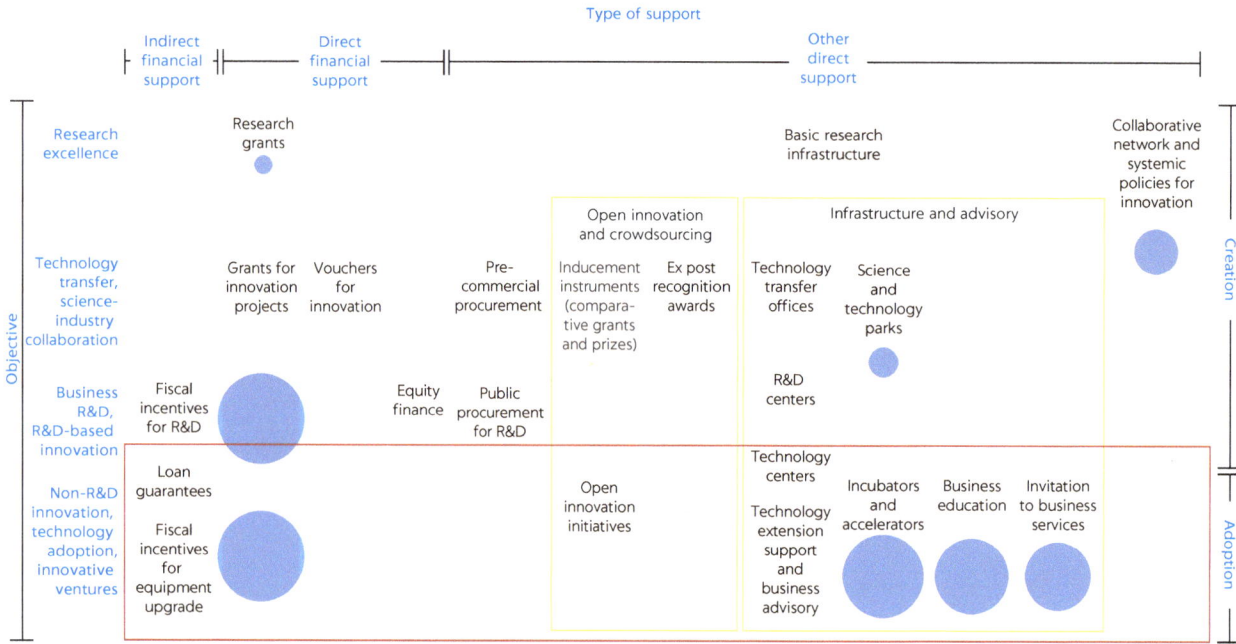

Source: Cruz et al. 2021.
Note: The size of each bubble is proportionate to total funding. R&D = research and development.

FIGURE 4.6

Sources of funding for public programs and intermediary organizations

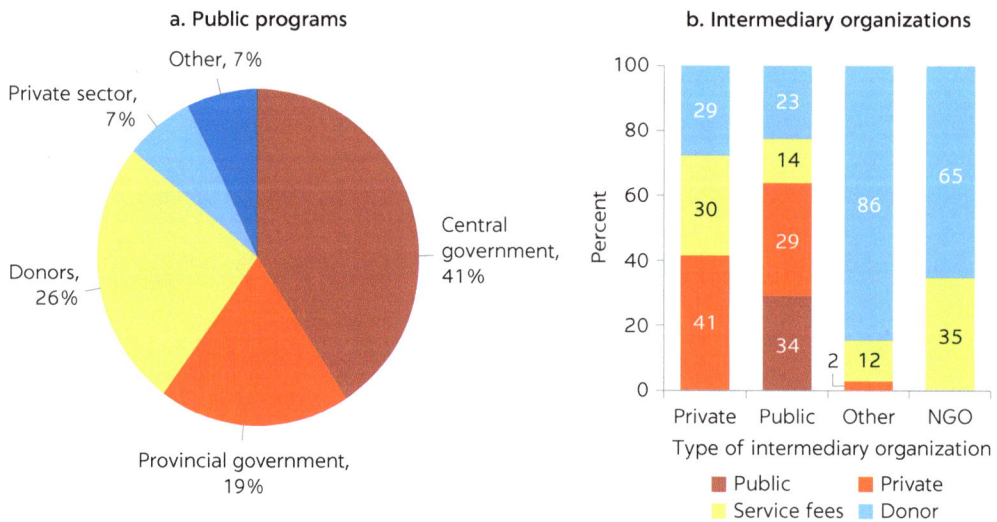

Source: Cruz and Hernandez Uriz 2022.
Note: Panel a is based on 20 observations and presents the percentage of programs receiving funding from each source. Panel b is based on the following number of observations: public, 12; private, 25; service fees, 30; donor, 28. NGO = nongovernmental organization.

understanding the existing ecosystem, as shown in figure 4.7, panel b. Each of these characteristics can also be related to one another (for example, broken down by sector) in the form of heatmaps (as in figure 4.4). As a result, such analysis can reveal whether support is concentrated among certain regions, sectors, firm types, and so on, thereby helping to identify gaps.

FIGURE 4.7

Entrepreneurship programs, by beneficiary

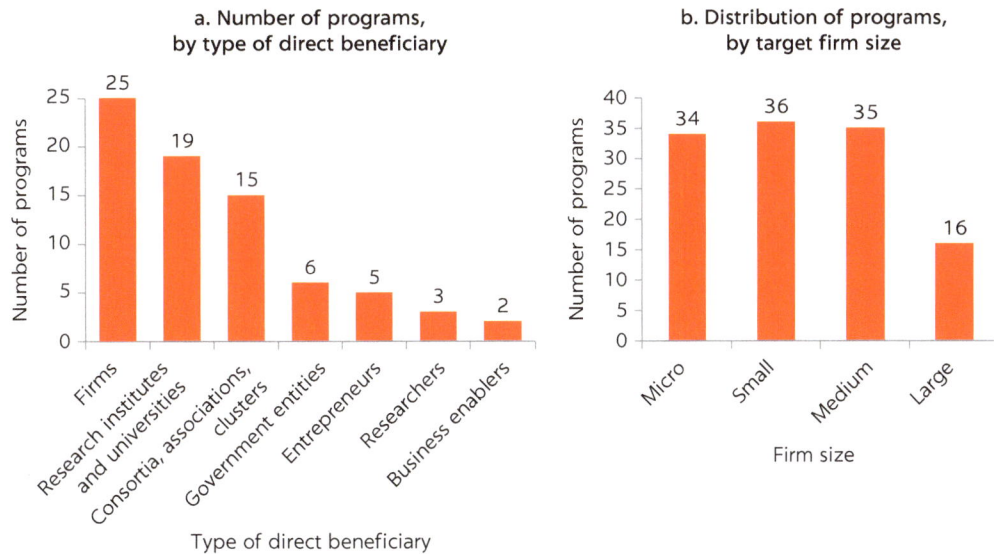

a. Number of programs, by type of direct beneficiary

b. Distribution of programs, by target firm size

Source: Cruz et al. 2021.

FIGURE 4.8

Management and M&E of support providers

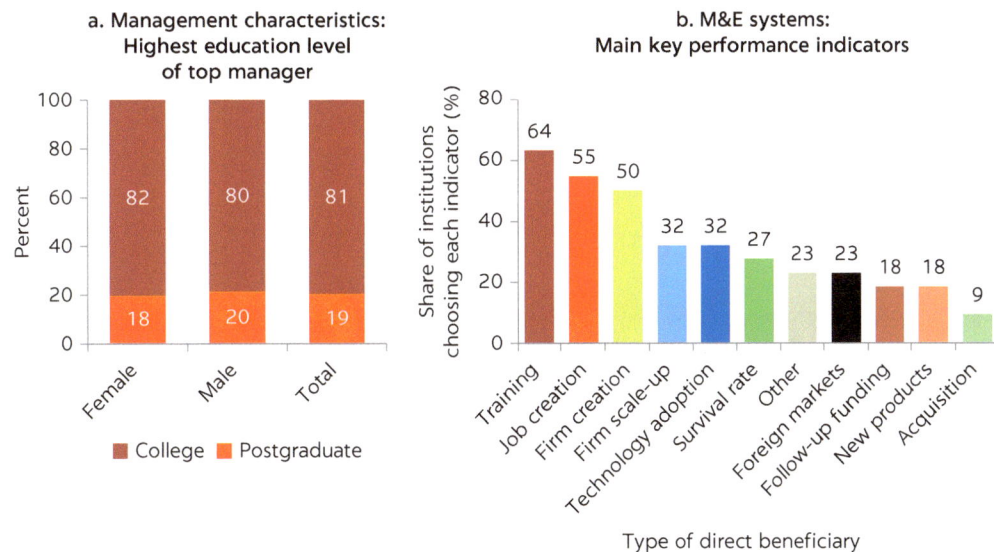

a. Management characteristics: Highest education level of top manager

b. M&E systems: Main key performance indicators

Source: Cruz and Hernandez Uriz 2022.
Note: Panel a is based on 26 observations; panel b is based on 22 observations. M&E = monitoring and evaluation.

The management characteristics and the M&E practices of public programs and IOs play a crucial role in the ecosystem. There are many dimensions of management that can be examined. Most commonly, teams can look into whether the top manager of a program or IO studied abroad (for example, for more than a month) and whether they helped start or owned a business themselves. The average years of work experience, age, and educational level can also be useful. Management characteristics are also typically broken down by gender (figure 4.8, panel a). For M&E, teams can look into whether any key performance indicators are measured (figure 4.8, panel b), how often they are measured, what type of indicators are measured, and whether impact evaluations are conducted.

4.5 SUMMARY OF THE POLICY MIX

After discussing public programs and IOs separately, the exercise should proceed with a summary and policy mix analysis combining the two, given that they play complementary roles in supporting entrepreneurship. The previous sections of the exercise provide a general overview of key features for public programs and IOs. Conversely, this section of the mapping exercise considers them together. First, it can summarize the results of the previous analysis and relate the findings to each other, for example, by comparing the relative coverage and key characteristics of public programs and IOs. Then, the section can analyze the complementarities between support provided by public programs and that provided by IOs. Particular attention should be paid to how suitable the current total policy mix is for addressing crucial gaps in the ecosystem. Finally, the analysis should identify the association across key characteristics of support interventions, aiming to provide an understanding of which main observable characteristics are associated with the provision of key services, depending on the country.

A first step in the total policy mix assessment is to combine and relate the previously analyzed information. For example, figure 4.9 shows the number of policies by the type of targeted outcome for both public programs and IOs. In this case, the figure reveals that IOs have a larger number of programs across most groups, but the public sector is still the main supporter of firm creation. Similarly, other direct comparisons between public programs and IOs can be presented in tables for important variables. These comparisons depend on the

FIGURE 4.9

Main outcomes targeted by public programs and IOs, by program type

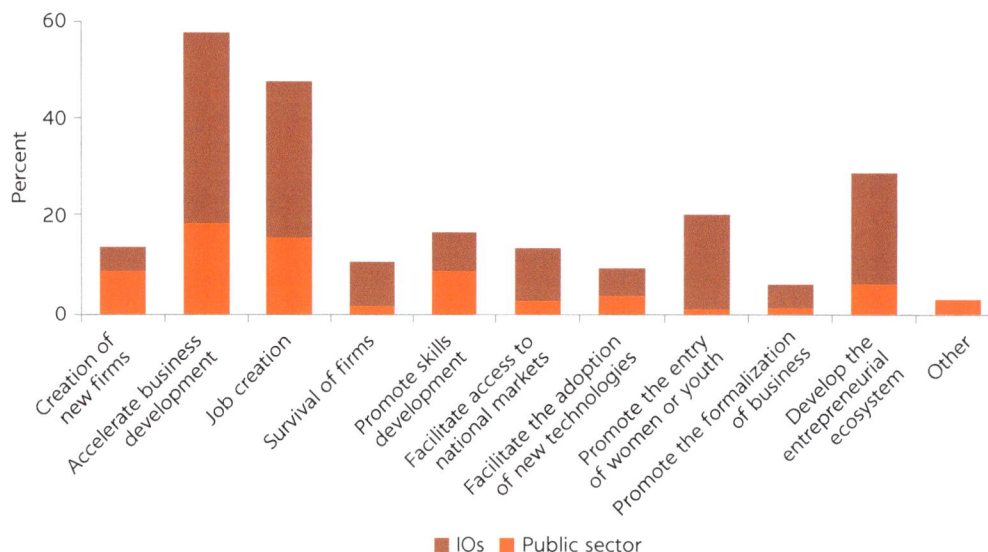

Source: Cruz and Hernandez Uriz 2022.
Note: IOs = intermediary organizations.

country context, but can often include the respective geographic distribution of policies, the adoption of impact evaluations in M&E processes, and so on.

Further, it is possible to use survey data to identify the key barriers from the perspective of IOs and public program managers, which helps characterize entrepreneurship support needs. First, teams can see which areas face the highest barriers and may need to be prioritized. Then, whether public program managers and IOs agree on the main needs can be analyzed. An example of such a comparison is given in figure 4.10. Because such information is rarely readily available, a survey might be implemented for this exercise.

Similarly, teams should seek to understand whether the existing supply of supporting actions is consistent with the perceived barriers and entrepreneurs' demand or whether there are gaps. As a result, policy suggestions can be made about which areas of support should be reduced or increased. This analysis should be performed for public programs and IOs separately, but also for the two combined. As an example, figure 4.11 shows this analysis for public programs and IOs in Kenya. It examines the relationship between services supplied (vertical axis) and the main identified barriers—which is used as a proxy for demand for those services (horizontal axis). Among other things, figure 4.11 shows that the support for access to markets appears relatively neglected compared with its perceived importance as a barrier. Further, the supply of services can be related to data on the policies desired by entrepreneurs if such data can be collected.

Teams should also analyze the association between key characteristics of public programs and IOs and their provided services. Although previous sections of the resulting report analyze key features of public programs and IOs, they do not describe the associations across these characteristics. Hence, the analysis should provide this link by focusing on three key questions: First, is the type of support associated with the size of programs, either by beneficiaries or

FIGURE 4.10

Barriers to entrepreneurship as perceived by ecosystem enablers

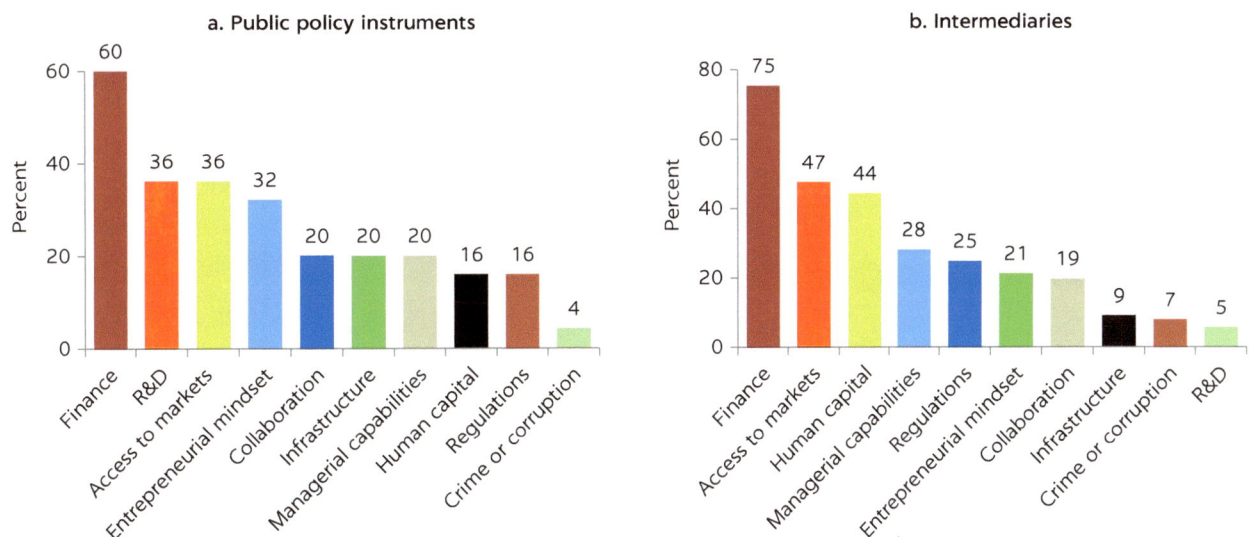

a. Public policy instruments

b. Intermediaries

Source: Cruz and Hernandez Uriz 2022.
Note: Panel a is based on 25 observations; panel b is based on 57 observations. R&D = research and development.

FIGURE 4.11

Supply of services versus demand for services due to main barriers identified by program managers

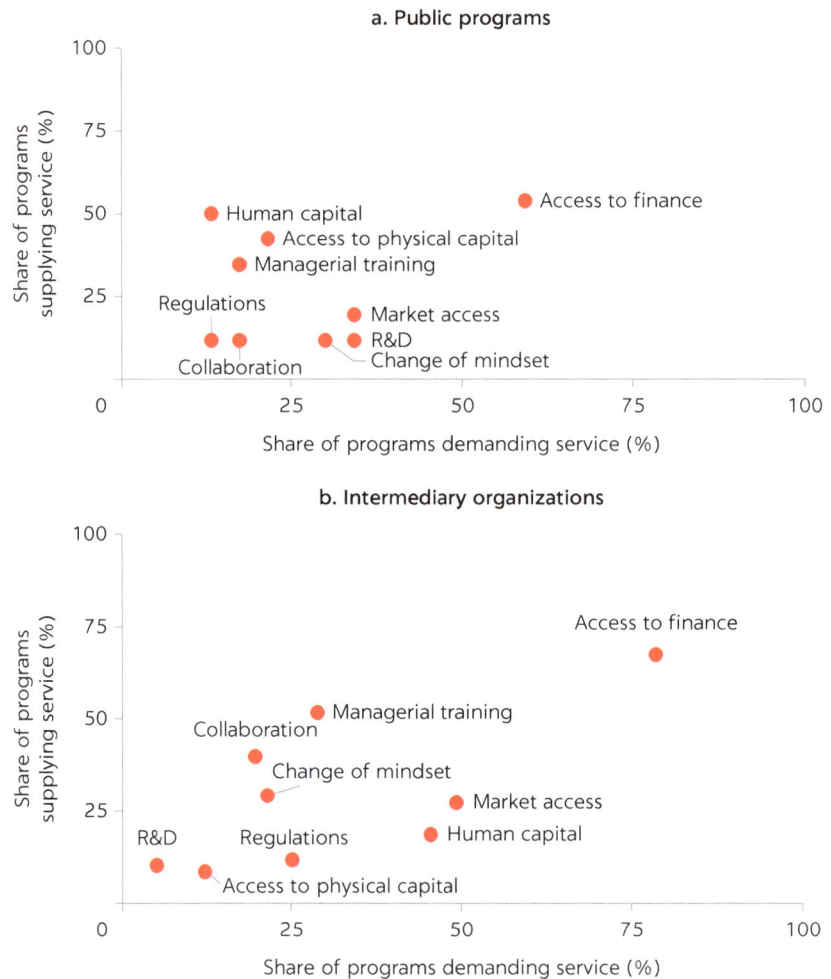

a. Public programs

b. Intermediary organizations

Source: Cruz and Hernandez Uriz 2022.
Note: R&D = research and development.

budget? Second, are there any further important characteristics associated with the different types of support offered? Third, are manager characteristics associated with any relevant features regarding M&E systems? However, the analysis to address these questions typically must rely on correlations because there is usually insufficient data for causal inference. In this context, simple descriptive exercises can provide some clarity on these relationships.

4.6 DATA COLLECTION PROCESS FOR MAPPING

The mapping exercise will usually use a mix of desk research, administrative data, and survey instruments, as well as alternative online data collection. Administrative data typically only apply to the public policy mix assessment. Surveys and web scraping, however, can be used for assessments of both public programs and IOs. Details on which variables to consider collecting for the public programs as well as implementation details for the surveys are given in online appendixes A and B, and alternative data collection is discussed in online appendix F. Data can be gathered from the following sources:

- *Administrative data.* National- and subnational-level data accumulated from secondary sources (official and proprietary data sets)
- *Survey instrument.* Respondent data collected using tools for policy mapping and IO mapping (see online appendixes A and B)
- *Online sources.* Web scraping of public online sources (see online appendix F) with a focus on social media, company websites, location data, government open data sites (if available), and other nontraditional data sources to augment information on IOs.

After identifying the relevant institutions that support entrepreneurship, teams can use the survey procedure described in online appendixes A and B to collect data from them. Because of a few key differences, separate questionnaires should be used for public programs and IOs, as described in the online appendixes. Each questionnaire can be downloaded using the links in the table of contents of this toolkit. The questionnaires would typically be submitted online to the organizations, with a follow-up by email or phone whenever necessary. These surveys provide the basis for a coherent and consistent analysis. They also aim to capture the quality of institutions supporting entrepreneurship. Specifically, the surveys assess institutions' structures, responsibilities, resources, and expenditures, as well as their impact M&E. Finally, the surveys include perceptions about the most important barriers in the ecosystem.

The data collection process should be led by a member of the World Bank team in collaboration with government counterparts. The processes for obtaining administrative data and conducting surveys need to be agreed upon with government counterparts. The government usually nominates focal points who become the main point of contact and assume responsibility for providing data as required. In addition, the counterparts should commit to building a first link between the World Bank country team and private organizations and institutions as well as nongovernmental organizations.

Data collection can be further enriched using nontraditional methods such as those listed below. For more details on alternative data collection, please refer to online appendix F.

- The list of institutions for the mapping stage can be augmented through web scraping methods. These lists can then be validated by subject matter experts and the local country team.
- Data gaps can be filled using online information such as the list of firms served by an accelerator or incubator throughout its lifetime.
- Multiple alternative sources can be used to check or triangulate traditionally gathered data. For instance, discrepancies between the data provided online and the survey responses can be noted.

NOTES

1. The figures and tables presented in this module are illustrative examples extracted from the pilot implemented in Kenya (Cruz and Hernandez Uriz 2022) and Romania (Cruz et al. 2021). For further details about the results, please consult the references.

2. The full Public Expenditure Review methodology is based on four stages: (1) inception report and policy mapping, (2) functional analysis, (3) efficiency analysis, and (4) effectiveness analysis. The factor "policy instruments" of the entrepreneurship assessment framework follows a similar approach. The policy mix assessment can be complemented by a functional analysis of the programs. See Andrews, Pritchett, and Woolcock (2012); Correa (2014); and Rasul and Rogger (2017) for further details on the Public Expenditure Review in Science, Technology, and Innovation methodology.

3. Online appendixes A through F are available at https://openknowledge.worldbank.org /handle/10986/40305.

4. The mapping of public programs can be complemented with the functional analysis to assess the quality of managerial and organizational practices in place. The World Bank has a wide set of diagnostics and well-established methodology for assessing public programs supporting science, technology, and innovation (Cirera et al. 2020; Correa 2014).

5. This list is based on desk research and interaction with private sector development specialists, and consists of public, nongovernmental, public-private, and private IOs.

REFERENCES

Andrews, Matt, Lant Pritchett, and Michael Woolcock. 2012. "Escaping Capability Traps through Problem-Driven Iterative Adaptation (PDIA)." Working Paper 299, Center for Global Development, Washington, DC.

Cirera, X., J. Frias, J. Hill, and Y. Li. 2020. *A Practitioner's Guide to Innovation Policy: Instruments to Build Firm Capabilities and Accelerate Technological Catch-Up in Developing Countries.* Washington, DC: World Bank.

Correa, Paulo. 2014. *Public Expenditure Reviews in Science, Technology, and Innovation: A Guidance Note.* Washington, DC: World Bank.

Cruz, Marcio, and Zenaida Hernandez Uriz. 2022. *Entrepreneurship Ecosystems and MSMEs in Kenya.* Washington, DC: World Bank. https://doi.org/10.1596/38230.

Cruz, Marcio, Natasha Kapil, Pablo Andres Astudillo Estevez, Christopher David Haley, Zoe Cordelia Lu, and Pelin Arslan. 2021. *Starting Up Romania: Entrepreneurship Ecosystem Diagnostic.* Washington, DC: World Bank. http://documents.worldbank.org/curated /en/099920106072238493/P174325083a5cc0eb090350dcde4c6a32df.

Rasul, I., and D. Rogger. 2017. "Management of Bureaucrats and Public Service Delivery: Evidence from the Nigerian Civil Service." *Economic Journal* 128 (608): 413–46. doi:10.1111 /ecoj.12418.

Digital Market Regulations

5.1 INTRODUCTION

Digital market regulations play a critical role for businesses engaging in the digital economy (World Bank 2021). Enabling regulations for traditional entrepreneurship, such as ease of starting a business or business-friendly licensing requirements, are necessary but not sufficient for digital businesses.

This module aims to address the following questions:

- What is the current stage of digital regulations in the country?
- What are the relevant dimensions to be analyzed with respect to digital market regulations?
- What are the key bottlenecks to updating digital regulations in the face of country priorities?

A sample structure of a country assessment of digital market regulation is provided in box 5.1.

5.2 A CONCEPTUAL FRAMEWORK FOR ASSESSING DIGITAL MARKET REGULATIONS

An assessment of digital market regulations needs to consider laws and policies that encourage the creation, entry, and adoption of digital and disruptive technologies. The combination of these dimensions allows innovations and new business models to scale up while ensuring equitable distribution and contestability in digital markets (figure 5.1).

A comprehensive assessment of digital market legislation is needed for several reasons. First, existing legislation may not be suitable given that it was designed for an "offline" economy. For example, existing consumer protection or taxation laws may fail to capture digital products and services. Second, as outlined above, the digital economy is characterized by distinct dynamics such as winner-takes-most tendencies that call for an update of countries' competition policy tools. For example, existing competition law may not properly account for

Box 5.1

Country assessment of digital market regulation: Sample structure (based on pilots in Nigeria and Vietnam)

A. Introduction

B. Digital market regulation framework: Adopt-scale-equity

C. Landscape of digital businesses
   1. Overview
   2. Brief overview of selected digital subsectors common in developing countries
      a. E-commerce
      b. Fintech
      c. Travel tech
      d. Gig economy (in particular, ride-sharing and food delivery)
      e. Software industry

D. Regulatory environment for digital business models (prioritize according to local context, including enforcement capabilities)
   1. E-transactions
      a. National laws on e-transactions (within each regulatory area)
      b. Main regulatory gaps and areas of reform (within each regulatory area)

   2. Personal data protection
   3. Cybersecurity and cybercrime law
   4. Online consumer protection
   5. Online supplier protection
   6. Competition policy and contestable digital markets
   7. Intellectual property rights
   8. Public procurement
   9. Open data policy and industry data sharing
   10. Cross-border data transfers
   11. Taxation of digital activities
   12. Regulations for gig economy platforms (such as ride-sharing and accommodation-sharing)

E. Summary of key challenges and recommendations (for example, a heatmap of the 12 topics above to understand major gaps)

Reference

Online Appendix D, "Market Regulations of Digital Businesses," available at https://openknowledge.worldbank.org/handle/10986/40305.

Source: Summary from various country pilots on digital market regulation assessments.

antitrust cases in which a digital conglomerate blurs traditional market definition by using its data from one market to exert dominance in another market (economies of scope).[1] Similarly, countries may not yet have regulations that address issues faced by digital start-ups that are highly dependent on large "gatekeeper" platforms for selling their products and services (such as app stores, operating systems, or social media platforms). Third, digital start-ups must comply with a set of digital market regulations that govern aspects of the digital economy, including cybersecurity, data protection, and electronic transaction laws. Substantial assistance is needed for start-ups (or even government agencies) on enforcement and keeping compliance costs within a reasonable range while still delivering the policy objectives, especially given the constraints faced by developing economies.

A strategic market segmentation approach can help policy makers identify which parts of a value chain are most affected by the digitalization trend and therefore need regulatory attention. This approach would help improve the accuracy and efficacy of regulatory interventions. See box 5.2 for more details.

FIGURE 5.1

The "adopt-scale-equity" regulatory framework for digital businesses

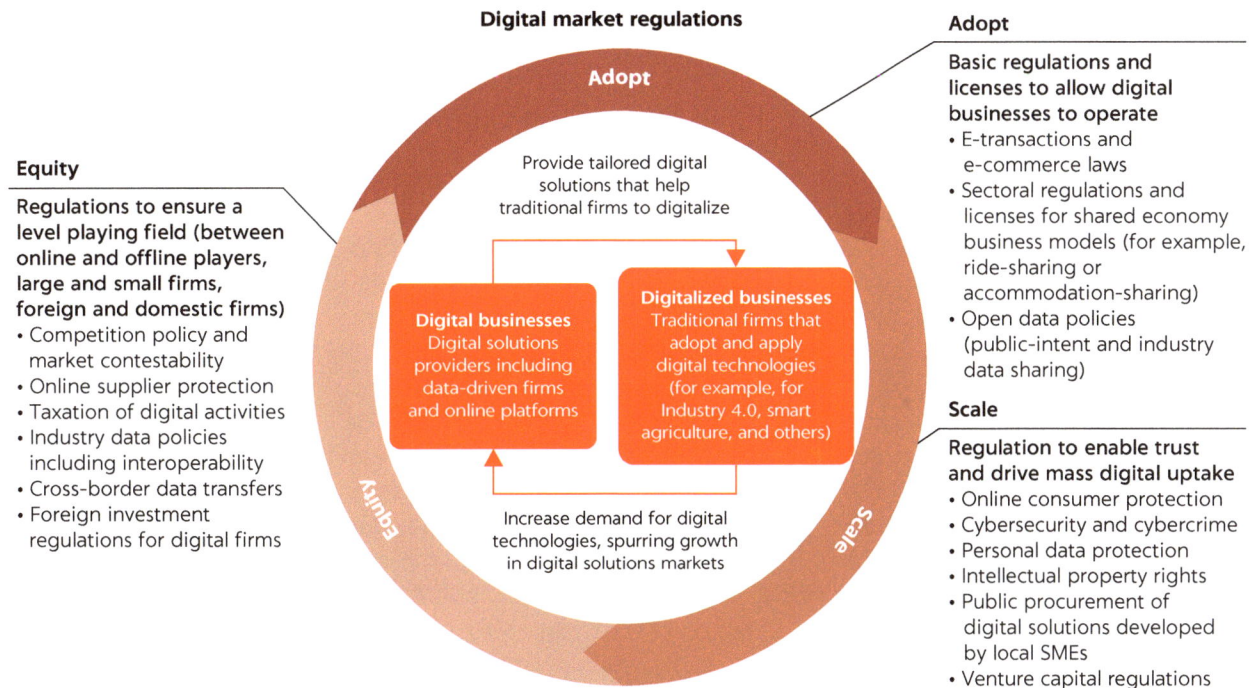

Source: Adapted from Akhlaque et al. 2022.
Note: Please also see other regulatory frameworks related to the digital economy that cut across some of these dimensions but have different emphases (for example, Daza Jaller and Molinuevo 2020; World Bank 2021). SMEs = small and medium enterprises.

Box 5.2

Strategic market segmentation of digitalized industries: Identifying implications for regulatory policy

A strategic market segmentation perspective highlights the changes that value chains undergo as a result of digitalization and helps derive regulatory implications for policy making for digital entrepreneurship. Although many market assessments define segments by associating them with specific products, strategic segments are defined by both a solution and the end user that the solution serves. For example, rather than defining "automobile parts" as a segment, a strategic segmentation may focus on mobility solutions for customers in either urban or rural areas. More important, such an approach can help governments assess which segments of a value chain have been greatly affected by the digital technologies and therefore deserve regulatory attention. Two examples follow from the ground transport and nutraceutical sectors.

Example 1—Ground passenger transport industry

Before being disrupted by digitalization, competitiveness in traditional market segments of the ground passenger transport industry (such as short-distance individual transport) would be defined by aspects such as vehicle design, performance, driving experience, fuel efficiency, emissions reduction, and level of customization. Digitalization shifted the paradigm to mobility as a service, including ride-sharing or car sharing and new mobility solutions such as autonomous vehicles. Market segmentation based on products and their supply chain would not provide sufficient intelligence for a firm's or country's competitiveness. Digitalization has created entirely new entrants and changed the factors determining competitiveness. For example, traditional car

continued

manufacturers now need to compete on multiple fronts, including with mobility providers (such as Didi, Uber, and Zipcar), tech giants (such as Apple and Google), and emerging original equipment manufacturers (such as BYD and Tesla).

This shift has multiple implications for policy makers. Competitiveness in the mobility industry today depends not just on state-of-the-art vehicle manufacturing but also on firms' access to high-quality and updated geospatial data, advanced cyber-security and computing capabilities, data protection safeguards, and the ability to securely transfer large amounts of data across borders. Moreover, it complicates the competitive landscape that antitrust authorities need to oversee and alters responsibilities around product liability and safety. (For example, software updates are critical for the safety of interconnected vehicles.) Given the scale of interconnectedness, competitiveness in the digitalized mobility industry depends increasingly on the ability of market participants to meet established industry standards that allow them to integrate their products into global value chains (for example, car-to-car communication protocols, cybersecurity standards, data standards for geospatial and personal information, and consumer safety).

Example 2—Nutraceuticals industry

Nutraceuticals are nutritional supplements that consumers either need (because of an underlying medical condition) or want (for health or cosmetic benefits). The regulation of nutraceuticals varies by jurisdiction (for example, regulated as drugs, as nutritional supplements, as food, or unregulated), and they are usually distributed over the counter. Nutraceuticals are usually mass produced and bought either based on an individual's own assessment or following a prescription from a medical professional—usually involving a test at an accredited medical laboratory.

Digitalization in combination with advancements in medical technology has led to the emergence of a more personalized market for nutraceuticals in which firms offer a range of diagnostics based on which a customized nutraceutical product is made. Diagnostics may range from rudimentary self-assessments through online forms to users mailing self-administered blood or stool samples to private laboratories for genome sequencing or other tests. The test results may make the difference between nutraceuticals that are medically required or a voluntary addition. Competitiveness of nutraceutical companies may depend not only on manufacturing such medications but also on their ability to use new business models for their advantage. Whereas this segment was previously mostly confined to individuals interacting with health care institutions, nutraceutical companies may now directly interact with patients or customers.

This new opportunity due to advances in technology also creates new business partnership models across industries given that it could be beneficial for nutraceutical companies to partner with ride-sharing or food delivery platforms for high-convenience delivery of test kits and products; meanwhile, however, it creates new regulatory challenges for governments. For example, governments need to determine how to appropriately assess the quality and accuracy of these digitalized or semi-digitalized tests carried out by the nutraceutical companies and how to certify and accredit them. In addition, how can fair competition between the new players and the traditional health care institutions be ensured, given that they bear different levels of risk? All these issues need to be addressed to gain consumers' trust and to properly nurture this new industry.

5.3 A STRUCTURED SURVEY FOR ASSESSING DIGITAL MARKET REGULATIONS

An assessment of the regulatory framework needs to cover both the de jure provisions as well as their de facto implementation. In a rapidly changing technological context, it is good regulatory practice to define legal requirements using broader objectives to prevent laws from becoming outdated too quickly once technology advances (that is, the technology neutrality principle). If government authorities lack the capacity or expertise to define legal requirements in this way, there may be a regulatory vacuum in some areas, overregulation in others, and overall, a high degree of legal uncertainty that may deter digital growth, and could also increase the risk of innovation-hindering political favoritism through the creation of artificial entry barriers for disruptive start-ups to challenge the incumbents.

Assessments of gaps in countries' overarching legal frameworks for digital markets can build on the World Bank's "digital market regulation survey," which provides a set of qualitative and standardized questions on 13 regulatory areas with relevance to digital businesses (see box 5.3). The questionnaire can be used by legal or policy experts to record the current regulatory landscape in a country based on desk research and expert interviews. The questions used in the

---

Box 5.3

Questionnaire topics on digital market regulations that policy makers can choose to examine

See online appendix D for a structured survey with questions on the topics below.

1. E-transactions (for example, equivalence of digital records and signatures, e-payments, e-customs, and e-logistics)
2. Personal data protection (for example, regulations on collection and processing of personal data, sensitive personal information)
3. Cross-border data transfers and localization requirements (for example, restrictions on the transfer of personal data to a foreign country)
4. Cybersecurity and cybercrime (for example, regulations that criminalize unauthorized access to data systems or content-related crimes such as fake news)
5. Consumer protection for online transactions (for example, prohibition of unfair contract terms, required disclosure of information during online transactions, intermediary liability of digital platforms)

6. Online supplier requirements and protection (for example, permits required for any regulated activities transacted online, protections for individuals supplying goods and services through a digital platform)
7. Competition policy and contestable digital markets (for example, application of competition law to the digital economy including market definition and abuse of dominance, merger control)
8. Intellectual property protection and public procurement of digital services (for example, specific provisions on digital businesses such as licensing infringements, equal access of digital businesses to government procurement contracts)
9. Digital taxation and harmonization (for example, registration and tax requirements for foreign-owned digital businesses, obligations

continued

Box 5.3, *continued*

of digital platforms to provide transaction information for tax purposes)

10. Regulations on accommodation-sharing platforms (for example, specific regulations such as zoning rules or licenses, requirements regarding screening of hosts and guests)

11. Regulations on ride-sharing platforms (for example, insurance and background

requirements for transport networking companies, provisions on social security)

12. Regulations on gig economy platforms (for example, requirement that platforms check qualifications of gig economy workers, social security provisions)

13. Open data policies (for example, access to public-intent data)

questionnaire have been harmonized with other relevant tools to the extent possible (for example, Data Policy surveys for *World Development Report 2021* [World Bank 2021] and MENA Tech [Daza Jaller and Molinuevo 2020]) to allow for benchmarking. It also includes de facto questions. Note that it is not compulsory for countries to conduct analyses on all 13 topics. Depending on the type of digital business activities and issues faced in a country, policy makers can choose to evaluate specific aspects. This survey provides a menu of regulatory topics and key evaluation questions that affect digital businesses.

After assessing gaps in digital market regulations, policy recommendations must consider the sequencing of reforms based on the specific country context. For example, e-transaction laws provide a crucial foundation for any digital solutions to be offered because they clarify the legal validity of electronic documents, contracts, and signatures. In a similar way, personal data may not be properly protected if there are no legal obligations concerning the cybersecurity of information and communication technology systems—if personal data are not secure, they cannot be protected properly.

Digital payment regulations are also key enabling policies for driving digital economy growth, although the topic is not covered in this toolkit. According to the World Bank Global Findex database, in developing economies, the share of adults making or receiving digital payments grew from 35 percent in 2014 to 57 percent in 2021, with the COVID-19 (coronavirus) pandemic further catalyzing this growth (see Demirguc-Kunt et al. [2018] for further details on the dynamics pre-COVID 19). In high-income economies, the share of adults making or receiving digital payments is nearly universal (95 percent). Digital payment and mobile money are a gateway to using other financial and digital services, enabling digital economy growth and financial inclusion. Informality, geographic barriers, volatile income, and digital finance literacy are some commonly cited demand-side barriers, whereas high operating costs, legacy business models, and limited competition and innovation are examples of supply-side barriers. The World Bank has published extensive tools, databases, and reports on this topic (see, for example, Pazarbasioglu et al. [2020] on digital financial services; Natarajan and Balakrishnan 2020 on fast payment systems).

Although matters concerning contestability in digital markets have attracted attention more recently, developing economies should not consider them to be an afterthought of digital market development. Regulations on competitive digital markets are key when aiming to nurture an ecosystem that allows new digital start-ups to emerge, scale up, and compete with incumbents. Equitable digital markets provide the context for new and innovative digital start-ups to emerge without innovation being disrupted by rent-seeking incumbents.

In addition to sequencing digital market regulations, it is critical for policy makers to apply an agile regulatory approach that is principle-based and proportional to risks, using new enforcement tools to be more effective in rapidly changing digital markets. The high degree of dynamism in the digital economy calls for agile approaches that build on principles rather than prescribing detailed technical solutions. For example, legislation that states regulatory objectives will be more effective than mandates for the use of specific technical solutions (such as numeric passwords, given that the technological status quo has since shifted to more secure biometric ways of authentication). Instead, the government may support companies by offering voluntary technical guidelines such as standards (for example, for cybersecurity) that can be updated more frequently than legislation to reflect the technological reality and that support market participants' compliance with broadly defined policy objectives (such as ensuring the security of information systems).

5.4 COUNTRY CASE PILOTS OF DIGITAL MARKET REGULATIONS ASSESSMENT

In many areas it may be more effective for policy makers to focus their efforts on strengthening the enforcement of existing legislation rather than enacting new legislation. For example, even though existing consumer protection legislation may be sufficient to cover online commerce, its implementation may be improved by setting up systems that support consumers by defending their rights in a manner that reflects the features of online transactions versus offline ones (for example, via online dispute resolution mechanisms, see box 5.4, or by updating existing competition policies to reflect the nature of new digital business models, see box 5.5).[2] Moreover, additional guidance documents on how existing rules apply to digital settings may also be required and could contribute to the better application of regulations.[3]

Box 5.4

Case study: Online dispute resolution mechanisms in Vietnam

A World Bank digital market regulation assessment in Vietnam found that the country's consumer protection legislation is largely applicable for online transactions. However, its implementation may require updating to meet the specific challenges of online transactions, especially to increase enforcement capacity and consumer awareness and to deal with cross-border transactions. This focus was in line with the government's goals outlined in the *National Master Plan for E-Commerce Development* for 2021–25, which describes the development of policies to settle disputes, encourages setting up independent dispute settlement systems, and supports participating in regional and international online dispute settlements (Socialist Republic of Vietnam 2020).

The World Bank provided the Vietnam Ministry of Industry and Trade with policy support for setting up an online dispute resolution (ODR) mechanism,

continued

Box 5.4, *continued*

in particular by referencing international good practices (for example, from Brazil, China, the European Union, the Republic of Korea, Singapore, and Thailand). ODR mechanisms rely on the use of information and communication technology (ICT) to bring together buyers and sellers and aim to resolve disputes through mediation and arbitration. The ICT systems allow ODR mechanisms to deal with a large number of small-value consumer complaints, which are characteristic of e-commerce (in Vietnam, the average e-commerce basket is worth about 340,000 Vietnamese dong [equivalent to US$17]; Statista 2021). ODR systems promise fast and easy dispute resolution and have therefore been set up by individual platforms and nongovernmental organizations as well as by governments around the world. The US

e-commerce platform eBay, for example, is often referred to as a forerunner in setting up a private ODR system through which it processed more than 60 million cases in 2015 (Rule 2017).

Given the e-commerce challenge of many small-value transactions, current Vietnamese consumer protection measures do not sufficiently support consumers. Concerns about security and transaction errors are the leading reasons for low uptake of digital payment methods, likely keeping Vietnamese consumers from making higher-value purchases online. So far, the ways for consumers in Vietnam to address issues related to cross-border transactions, for example, with ASEAN (Association of Southeast Asian Nations) countries, are limited.

Source: Adapted from World Bank 2022.

Box 5.5

Case study: Digital market contestability regulatory revisions in Nigeria

A World Bank digital market regulation assessment in Nigeria identified significant developments and important steps toward improving the ease of doing business and ensuring market contestability and competition in Nigeria. In 2019, Nigeria took an important step by passing the Federal Competition and Consumer Protection Act (FCCPA) and creating the Federal Competition and Consumer Protection Commission (FCCPC). Given the intricate task of enforcing antitrust provisions in digital markets, the World Bank assessment recommended to Nigerian policy makers that they develop guidelines that support implementation of the FCCPA. For example, guidelines may provide clarity on how authorities are to define digital markets given that new digital business models render traditional market boundaries obsolete (for example, because of economies of scope) and how to assess an abuse of dominance (for example, deciding whether to

introduce provisions that prohibit unfair actions ex ante, or defining relative versus absolute market dominance positions).

The FCCPC issued merger review regulations that define when merger notifications are required. This regulatory update is considered an important step toward improving the regulatory environment for digital entrepreneurship because it enables the FCCPC to review mergers that under the previous threshold would have not been captured. Areas that were identified include improving the thresholds for notification of small mergers and developing the criteria to review small mergers that would otherwise not meet notification thresholds. The inclusion of such clarifications would ensure that harmful transactions in the digital space are identified by the competition authority even if the turnover of the target is not significant.

Source: Adapted from Zottel et al. 2021.

NOTES

1. Note, for example, that the European Commission is revising its 1997 Notice on Market Definition. This point is one of the issues considered (European Commission 2021).
2. In addition to policy makers, there can also be a role for civil society and consumer organizations to engage in advocacy and make consumers aware of their rights.
3. Examples in the context of EU consumer law are four notices from the European Commission in December 2021 (European Commission, n.d.).

REFERENCES

Akhlaque, Asya, Shawn Weiming Tan, Tingting Juni Zhu, and Philip Grinsted. 2022. "Digital Market Regulations for Promoting Business Innovation and Digitalization in Vietnam." World Bank Group, Washington, DC. https://documents1.worldbank.org/curated /en/099755006152227000/pdf/P1595780ec45e20bf09f6308da9d054ef29.pdf.

Daza Jaller, Lillyana Sophia, and Martin Molinuevo. 2020. "Digital Trade in MENA: Regulatory Readiness Assessment." Policy Research Working Paper 9199, World Bank, Washington, DC. http://documents.worldbank.org/curated/en/786271585574266618/Digital-Trade -in-MENA-Regulatory-Readiness-Assessment.

Demirguc-Kunt, A., L. Klapper, D. Singer, and S. Ansar. 2018. *The Global Findex Database 2017: Measuring Financial Inclusion and the Fintech Revolution.* Washington, DC: World Bank.

European Commission. n.d. "Review of EU Consumer Law." Accessed March 22, 2023, https:// commission.europa.eu/law/law-topic/consumer-protection-law/review-eu -consumer-law_en.

European Commission. 2021. "Evaluation of the Commission Notice on the Definition of Relevant Market for the Purposes of Community Competition Law of 9 December 1997." Commission Staff Working Document SWD (2021) 199 final, European Commission, Brussels.

Natarajan, H., and M. Balakrishnan. 2020. "Real-Time Retail Payments System or Faster Payments: Implementation Considerations." *Journal of Payments Strategy and Systems* 14 (1): 48–60.

Pazarbasioglu, C., A. G. Mora, M. Uttamchandani, H. Natarajan, E. Feyen, and M. Saal. 2020. "Digital Financial Services." World Bank, Washington, DC.

Rule, Colin. 2017. "Designing a Global Online Dispute Resolution System: Lessons Learned from eBay." *University of St. Thomas Law Journal* 13 (2): 354.

Socialist Republic of Vietnam. 2020. "On Approving the National Master Plan for E-Commerce Development in the Period of 2021–2025." Decision No. 645/QD-TTg. Enacted 15 May 2020.

Statista. 2021. "Value of an Average E-Commerce Basket in Southeast Asia in 2020, by Country (in U.S. Dollars)." *E-Commerce.* https://www.statista.com/statistics/1231732/sea -average-e-commerce-basket-value-by-country/?locale=en.

World Bank. 2021. *World Development Report 2021: Data for Better Lives.* Washington, DC: World Bank. https://www.worldbank.org/en/publication/wdr2021.

World Bank. 2022. "Online Consumer and Supplier Protection: Addressing Challenges through Digital-Enabled Enforcement Tools." Regulatory Brief for the Government of Vietnam. World Bank, Washington, DC.

Zottel, Siegfried, Tingting Juni Zhu, Ana Cristina Alonso Soria, and Yoon Keongmin. 2021. "Regulatory Analysis: Digital Entrepreneurship in Nigeria." World Bank Group, Washington, DC. https://documents1.worldbank.org/curated/en/099062823151013200/pdf/P16739908 8635b0260b2e3061ffffaf10f6.pdf.

3 Policy

Policy Options to Support Entrepreneurial Ecosystems

6.1 INTRODUCTION

The entrepreneurial ecosystem assessment should be finalized with a validation exercise and a plan for implementing policy recommendations based on diagnostics. This module aims to provide policy makers and practitioners with a process that allows them to define priorities for policy direction informed by the analysis conducted in the previous modules. For each prioritized area, the analysis should then recommend specific policy instruments, considering the current policy mix identified in module 4. Whenever this work is led by the World Bank, the analysis could indicate which financial instruments would be the best options for tackling these issues.

This module aims to address the following questions:

- What instruments are available to support entrepreneurial ecosystems?
- What evidence supports these instruments?
- How can the findings be validated, and how can qualitative information be obtained from stakeholders to define policy priorities?
- How can the information proposed in this toolkit be used for recommending and evaluating policies?

A sample structure for this analysis is provided in box 6.1.

6.2 POLICY INTERVENTIONS TO SUPPORT AN ECOSYSTEM

The policy priorities to support entrepreneurial ecosystems should be informed by the results of the assessment and validated by stakeholders. Policy makers need to carefully analyze their ecosystems and judge whether the benefits of particular interventions are worth the costs. Many instruments that are effective in one context may not be in another. Further, some instruments need to be used as part of a suite of interventions, and complementarities across interventions need to be assessed. For example, access to finance may be ineffective if nothing is done to stimulate entrepreneurs to enter the market.

Box 6.1

Policy options to support entrepreneurial ecosystems: Proposed structure

A. Introduction
B. Summary of the main findings from the validation exercise
C. Validation exercise
    1. Focus groups
    2. Intervention mechanisms

D. Policy recommendations
    1. Key policy priority
    2. Implementation timeline

E. Evaluation

As a first step, the overall policy objective can be based on the results of the cross-country analysis. As discussed, the cross-country analysis will reveal the areas in which a country is lagging at the national level of ecosystem outputs or pillars. For example, a country may be generating a lot of new firms but lag in the number of high-potential ones, meaning policies should focus on innovation and scale-up rather than entry of new firms. Similarly, the analysis on entrepreneurship pillars can indicate which pillars policy makers could prioritize given that some will be more important than others. The cross-country analysis can also help with the crafting of policies at a national level, especially for factors that are common across all firms or entrepreneurs.

The subnational analysis can then be used to further tailor and target policies. Having identified the areas in which a country is underperforming overall, it is important for policies to account for performance heterogeneity across ecosystems in those areas. In particular, a country may exhibit several local ecosystems at varied stages of development, each of which requires different types of policies. In this case, the subnational analysis helps by first identifying and then characterizing a country's relevant local ecosystems. For example, one ecosystem may be particularly crucial to improving a country's lagging innovation outputs. Similarly, different regions, sectors, or firms may require different policy priorities across the ecosystem pillars.

Proposed policies at all levels should consider the results of the policy mapping exercise. It is important to consider the current mix of policies and support from intermediary organizations (IOs) when suggesting new policies. A key consideration is whether current policies are addressing the identified constraints at the national and local levels. Similarly, teams should first consider whether existing policies can be adjusted and, if so, how that should be done. Further, teams should address any overlaps or gaps in the policy mix, considering the supply and demand for policies as well as the perceived and factual barriers to entrepreneurship. Often, such an assessment of the current policy mix indicates opportunities for merging programs and improving prioritization.

Policy makers have a wide range of potential instruments with which to support different aspects of entrepreneurship, which can be categorized in different ways. This section outlines some tools under the different elements of the entrepreneurial ecosystem framework presented in the introduction to this toolkit, including the following:

- Social capital and entrepreneurial characteristics
- Training to improve firm capabilities and human capital
- Facilitating market access
- Access to finance
- Taxation and regulatory framework
- Support infrastructure, including for knowledge capital
- Physical capital and infrastructure.

A crucial consideration in choosing priority areas is to determine the market or policy failures that warrant an intervention and the priority for intervention. Teams must clearly understand and articulate the market or policy failures that the project should solve. Table 6.1 presents some policy options based on the entrepreneurial ecosystem framework. It describes each area of available policy tools, notes the failures that it tries to solve, provides some examples and instruments that can be used to solve such constraints, and describes some evidence as well as success and failure factors.

The description and summary of the evidence presented in table 6.1 are based on several publications that provide results associated with the topic or summarize the literature with respect to key findings. These references could be used as a starting point for practitioners implementing the diagnostics, but this is not an exhaustive list. Some academic initiatives, such as VoxDev (see https://voxdev.org/voxdevlit), are providing up-to-date revision of the literature and evidence related to several topics. As of August 2023, they include training for entrepreneurs, microfinance, mobile money, informality, and agricultural technology in Africa, among other topics, including climate adaptation. These reviews are curated by leading scholars with outstanding knowledge on these topics, and we strongly recommend these materials.

Entrepreneurial ecosystem development stage

Policy priorities at the local level should be chosen based on the binding constraints given the development stage of the local ecosystem. In many cases, the same policy tool needs to be applied differently if used at different levels of ecosystem development. For example, access to finance during the nascent stage tends to focus on providing entrepreneurs with grants and microcredit loans; during the growth stage it focuses on promoting the creation of early-stage financing (such as angel investment networks); and during the consolidation stage, it helps with the establishment of more specialized financing options such as venture capital (VC) funds, funds of funds, or corporate venture funds. Understanding the key stages of development in an entrepreneurial ecosystem is important for proposing policies as well as for prioritizing actions. The following text describes the main characteristics of the development phases of an entrepreneurial ecosystem.

Nascent stage. Economic activity tends to agglomerate around spatial areas. The first step toward developing such agglomerations can be thought of as the nascent stage. This is the stage in which policy makers, entrepreneurs, universities, and different stakeholders start taking actions to diversify the economic activity and improve the sophistication of the types of products and services

TABLE 6.1 Summary of policy options for supporting entrepreneurial ecosystems

DESCRIPTION OF THE PROBLEM	MARKET OR POLICY FAILURES TO ADDRESS	SPECIFIC INSTRUMENTS AND EXAMPLES	EVIDENCE
Social capital and entrepreneurial characteristics			
The collective values, opinions, behaviors, and attitudes of the community toward entrepreneurs and entrepreneurship. Key factors include society's perception of status of entrepreneurs, attitude toward failure and risk-taking, and perception of skills required for entrepreneurial success.	Lack of information about what it means to be an entrepreneur, its benefits, risks, and challenges.

The policy objective is to provide people with knowledge so they can make an informed decision about whether to become an entrepreneur. | Entrepreneurship competitions and boot camps

Media (for example, TV shows, websites); promotion of local role models

Pre-entrepreneurship road shows and showcase events to raise basic awareness.

Business plan competitions

Hackathons

Training to improve entrepreneurs' personal initiative and perceptions | Evidence is mixed. Many programs target youth or population groups that tend not to be involved in firm creation and growth processes.

The impact on future firm creation is weak, although it can be relevant for marginalized populations.

Needs to address behavioral and cultural attitudes that are not easily moldable. |
| *Training to improve firm capabilities and human capital* | | | |
| Lack of entrepreneurial skills is a critical barrier to growth of entrepreneurship, particularly in developing economies.

Training is one of the main mechanisms that governments have implemented across developing economies. | Information costs and asymmetry: Entrepreneurs might not know the practices, processes, and skills they need to succeed and therefore might not invest in obtaining them. Also, it is costly for entrepreneurs to determine the quality of different service providers (such as consultants).

Policy objective: Setting up resources and infrastructure for imparting entrepreneurship skills training and supporting capacity development of entrepreneurs is a key tenet of any entrepreneurship promotion policy. | Management practices boot camps, workshops, and mentorship

Soft skills and leadership training

Access to networks of contacts

Access to incubation and acceleration programs

Study tours and placement of successful entrepreneurs in the entrepreneurial ecosystem

Creation of start-up hubs and promotion of knowledge-sharing platforms and business networks

Consulting and specialized services (productivity, exporting, digitalization, and so on) | Evidence on the impact of such trainings is mixed, but there is evidence that firms can significantly improve managerial practices through consulting services.

Quality of trainers and intervention matters.

A meta-analysis shows that the standard training model has modestly positive effects, on average, although the effects imply reasonably high returns on investments in training, given low costs per participant.

Although positive impacts are found, a cost-benefit analysis needs to be done in each case to evaluate whether the monetary value of the increase in profits would be cost-efficient. |

continued

TABLE 6.1, *continued*

DESCRIPTION OF THE PROBLEM	MARKET OR POLICY FAILURES TO ADDRESS	SPECIFIC INSTRUMENTS AND EXAMPLES	EVIDENCE
Facilitating market access			
Access and links to markets are critical to the growth of new firms and for attracting new entrepreneurs. There is often a strong policy focus on the supply side of entrepreneurship—encouraging new businesses—but far less focus on to whom these businesses need to sell to grow. In the absence of targeted policy-level interventions, new firms and young entrepreneurs may face more challenges to accessing customers, production inputs, and financing.	Externalities (learning effects): Exporting firms have been shown to increase productivity and improve quality of goods after entering new markets. High entry costs to engage in public procurement processes or to access new markets. The policy objective is to help entrepreneurs reach all their potential markets in the most efficient way, reducing transaction costs and generating externalities into other firms of the economy.	Antitrust laws, updating of competition policy, licensing policy Access to public procurement processes or preference in specific processes Open innovation programs with the public sector Export-promotion programs Landing pads or soft-landing programs for entrepreneurs accessing new countries	Evidence suggests that firms can benefit from access to external markets. Although direct access to monetary resources is coupled with other services, such interventions seem to have an impact on sales, profits, and the probability of getting new rounds of financing. Evidence on the impact of providing direct access to new markets specifically suggests that they can be effective. There is large evidence based on Latin American countries suggesting that export-promotion activities can benefit firms to entering the export market, as well as to grow. This evidence is also supported by cross-country analysis and randomized controlled trials in the Arab Republic of Egypt.
Access to finance			
Access to finance is critical to both new business establishment and growth. New and small businesses often do not have the financial track record or tangible assets to obtain financing or investments from financial institutions. Policy interventions may be used to facilitate access to different forms of financing for starting and scaling up businesses.	Information asymmetry: Lenders and investors do not have enough information about the venture. The policy objective is to provide financial resources to firms that are credit constrained so they can grow to their optimal level.	Provision of grants and subsidies Provision of credit and investment guarantees Expansion of supply of venture capital, equity funds, co-investment, and risk-sharing mechanisms to support start-ups Facilitation of provision of debt financing through banks or nonbanking financial institutions specializing in credit to SMEs Encouragement of crowdfunding	Overall, evidence on microfinance has not demonstrated transformational effects on key outcomes, such as profits and income. Yet, results are subject to significant variation across geographies, program design, and beneficiaries. Evidence from the Republic of Yemen suggests that matching grants targeting small firms can lead to more innovation, technology upgrade, and sales growth.

continued

TABLE 6.1, *continued*

DESCRIPTION OF THE PROBLEM	MARKET OR POLICY FAILURES TO ADDRESS	SPECIFIC INSTRUMENTS AND EXAMPLES	EVIDENCE
Taxation			
Taxation regime can have a significant impact on entrepreneurship by influencing an individual's or a firm's decision about whether to start a new business or seek employment, how much to invest in the growth and scaling up of the business, and whether to operate in the formal or the informal economy.	High taxation rates and inefficiencies might cause cash-flow constraints that hinder firm growth and investment decisions. Taxation inefficiencies and uncertainty about future taxation might cause people to avoid starting a business or encourage firms to remain informal. The policy objective is to provide a simple taxation system that considers the financial constraints faced by entrepreneurs in their first years and that provides certainty about future taxation rates.	Reduce the burden and cost of tax compliance. Provide exemptions from capital gains tax and expand permissible deductions for investors. Provide tax benefits for private sector partners and customers of start-ups.	Evidence from Brazil suggests that tax simplification programs, simplifying the tax system only for SMEs does not lead to higher formalization rate. Most of the existing evidence comes from quasi-experimental evaluations. In Europe, for example, results suggest that a reduction in the corporate tax rate would increase the entry rate of firms. However, the elasticity is higher in countries with better institutions, showing the effect of complementarities. In the intensive margin, taxation has also been correlated with lower quantity and quality of innovations in the United States.
Regulatory framework			
Business regulations inevitably lead to increased monetary and time costs for businesses. The cost of compliance is often disproportionately greater for small businesses, which, in turn, can inhibit entrepreneurial activity and encourage informal entrepreneurship. However, business regulations are necessary.	Some entrepreneurs might face regulatory constraints or voids due to the features of the innovative products or services provided by the firm. The policy objective is to reduce uncertainty and update regulations to meet the new characteristics of markets and goods provided to the economy while finding a balance in the level of regulation that encourages entrepreneurship within the formal economy without creating negative externalities in the business climate (such as fraud, exploitative behavior, and the like).	Easier procedure for business registration Regulatory sandbox to test disruptive new solutions Dedicated category of business incorporation for young firms and start-ups Less onerous corporate governance compliance framework Easier winding-up regime	Regulatory sandboxes ease the regulatory barriers or voids that new innovations can generate. Evidence on those mechanisms is new and sector specific. For example, UK fintech organizations that entered the sandbox were 50 percent more likely to raise funding than those that did not. This was more pronounced in small and young firms. Evaluations of the Italian Start-up Act find that participating in the program allows start-ups to get more financing, grow more, and be more likely to survive.

continued

TABLE 6.1, *continued*

DESCRIPTION OF THE PROBLEM	MARKET OR POLICY FAILURES TO ADDRESS	SPECIFIC INSTRUMENTS AND EXAMPLES	EVIDENCE
Support infrastructure for knowledge capital			
Entrepreneurial ecosystems include a range of support entities that entrepreneurs draw on for advice, guidance, networking, and connections. These can include incubators, accelerators, and coworking spaces; networks of advisers and mentors; and professional services (such as intellectual property lawyers). Support may be needed to establish these entities and to improve the quality of their offerings.	Coordination failures, missing markets, and agglomeration externalities can prevent a good venture from succeeding or cause it to leave the ecosystem because of the lack of support or missing actors in the ecosystem. The policy objective is to create markets of support services, provide quality information about service providers, and encourage the creation of clusters and networks that foster agglomeration externalities.	Creation of markets for consultants and support service providers Creation of or support for incubators, accelerators, and early-stage funds Financing of entrepreneurial ecosystem research Establishment, development, and support of knowledge parks, labs, and innovation centers	The evidence on programs aimed at creating or fostering knowledge or sectoral hubs is limited in most cases to observational studies of specific regions or sectors. Most of those studies show that the existence of hubs or programs attract new and more innovative entrepreneurs. Nevertheless, more work needs to be done in this area. Evidence shows that simply providing information about the value of those services does not affect the demand for them. However, providing firms with subsidies to access the market for consulting services increases the likelihood that firms will go back to the market for more services because they have experienced the benefits.
Physical capital and infrastructure			
Physical capital and infrastructure are key inputs and preconditions for firms to create and deliver products and services.	Missing markets: If the government does not invest in infrastructure (for example, energy, telecommunications, roads), it cannot be privately procured by a firm. Undersupply due to positive externalities: Because infrastructure is a public good that has positive spillovers to others, there will be insufficient private investment into it.	General access to infrastructure (for example, roads, internet, electricity) Creation of or support for incubators and accelerators that provide physical capital and infrastructure Creation of or support for business parks or special economic zones that provide infrastructure	Evidence on Africa suggests that improving digital infrastructure with the arrival of rapid internet has led to an increase in employment, firm entry rate, and productivity. Evidence from Chile suggests that providing basic infrastructure (for example, coworking space) with a bundled complementary service (for example, financing and training) may lead to increases in start-up fundraising. This effect is not observed for the basic service alone.

Sources: Original table for this publication based on the following references across the topics: Entrepreneurial culture and spirit—Alaref, Brodmann, and Premand 2020; Barsoum et al. 2022; Bjorvatn et al. 2020; Chioda et al. 2021; Frese, Gielnik, and Mensmann 2016; Peter and Pierk 2021; Robinson and Viceisza 2021. Training and capacity building—Assinova 2020; Cho and Honorati 2014; Gonzalez-Uribe and Reyes 2021; Iacovone, Maloney, and McKenzie 2019; McKenzie and Woodruff 2014, 2021; Piza et al. 2016. Facilitating market access—Cai and Szeidl 2018; Chatterji 2019; Cruz, Lederman, and Zoratto 2018; Monreal-Pérez and Geldres-Weiss 2019. Access to finance—Cornelli et al. 2020; De Mel, McKenzie, and Woodruff 2008; Goñi and Reyes 2019; McKenzie, Assaf, and Cusolito 2017; McKenzie and Woodruff 2008. Taxation—Akcigit et al. 2018; Da Rin, Di Giacomo, and Sembenelli 2011; Gentry and Hubbard 2000. Regulatory framework—Cornelli et al. 2021. Technology and innovation—Cirera, Cruz, and Comin 2022; Grover, Lall, and Maloney 2022; Gusberti et al. 2017; Kenney, Massini, and Murtha 2009; Viederyte 2016. Support infrastructure—Anderson and McKenzie 2021, 2022; Ezell and Atkinson 2011; Gardner and Henry, forthcoming; Gonzalez-Uribe and Leatherbee 2018; Hjort and Poulsen 2019. Regulatory climate—Biancalani, Czarnitzki, and Riccaboni 2022; Guerzoni, Nava, and Nuccio 2021.

Note: SMEs = small and medium-size enterprises.

produced in the area. The policy instruments around the nascent stage of an entrepreneurial ecosystem are focused on providing the minimum level of endowments so entrepreneurs' projects can start growing, including (1) promoting a culture around entrepreneurship and innovation, (2) creating a good business climate so people can see entrepreneurship as an economic activity with positive returns, (3) improving management and entrepreneurial skills, (4) providing access to basic infrastructure (such as roads and the internet), and (5) providing some grants or microcredits so entrepreneurs can start investing in improving their local offerings. The expected outcome of an intervention at this stage will be the minimum functioning of those factors. For example, it will be very unlikely that an entrepreneur can succeed, even with a good business idea and good skills, if access to the internet or to roads is limited or nonexistent. Similarly, an ecosystem with good infrastructure but with entrepreneurs with poor management skills and focused solely on the local market will not have many success stories.

Growth stage. Once an ecosystem is able to generate sufficient economic activity involving some level of innovation and sophistication, new people will become more interested in becoming entrepreneurs, or existing entrepreneurs will be encouraged to follow successful examples. Policy makers and ecosystem stakeholders can take advantage of those positive externalities to further develop the ecosystem. The main objective in this stage is to ensure that success stories are not isolated cases. Thus, policy makers need to change from offering basic services to entrepreneurs to offering more sophisticated services. Also in this stage, new support services and policies will need to be created so entrepreneurs of different backgrounds and sectors can succeed.

Specialization and consolidation stage. The growth of successful ecosystems tends to be biased toward certain sectors or skills, in part because of existing endowments (for example, geography, knowledge hubs, culture). Firms also start demanding more specialized human capital and suppliers as they grow, which encourages people and firms to relocate to the area to meet the demand while also generating positive spillovers. Many of those specialized workers will identify new business opportunities and start new firms. Suppliers will become more efficient as knowledge about the market improves. In addition, more specialized support services will be provided. Those sophisticated demands will need to be met by the correct infrastructure and support services, so the agglomeration benefits continue to be higher than the congestion costs.

The expected impact of any intervention will depend not only on the quality of the intervention, but also on a good targeting strategy and existing positive or negative complementarities. As such, no intervention should be seen in a vacuum, but rather as an enabler in a part of the ecosystem. Grover, Lall, and Maloney (2022) describe the importance of evaluating the mix of barriers to appraise the value of an intervention. For example, creating an angel investment network will not have the expected impact if there are not enough high-potential entrepreneurs in the market. Similarly, promoting the entrepreneurial culture in an ecosystem with a bad regulatory climate will not generate more entrepreneurship in the country. Consequently, it is important to understand policy instruments within each stage as policy mix options that could take an ecosystem from one stage to another.

Gradually rolling out new policies in strategic ecosystems can help maximize long-term benefits due to learning effects. To reduce the cost of implementation and increase the chances of spillovers, interventions should be piloted in high-potential ecosystems, which can benefit from economies of agglomeration to optimize potential spillover effects. By targeting specific local ecosystems and rolling out the program gradually (for example, digital ecosystems in one state, region, or city and agribusiness ecosystems in another), policy makers can learn about the impact of interventions using impact evaluations with counterfactual exercises and improve the implementation. Moreover, these activities could experiment with the use of digital tools and consulting based on groups of firms with similar characteristics and operating in similar environments.

6.3 FINANCIAL INSTRUMENTS FOR DIGITAL BUSINESSES AND TECH START-UPS

Among all relevant policy instruments, the country pilots have identified a large demand for improving access to finance for digital businesses and tech entrepreneurs. In addition to personal resources, crowdfunding, and grants, VC is a relevant source of funding for digital start-ups.[1] VC is a type of private equity financing at early-stage private companies. Given start-ups' low rate of business success, VC investments (box 6.2) are usually made by investors that have sufficient financial backing and the required expertise to gauge risks and bear the potential loss of their investment. In addition to VC financing and instruments such as crowdfunding or digital lending platforms, government grants may be an important financing source for digital start-ups. However, given smaller ticket sizes (about US$5,000–US$50,000), government grants play a role primarily at the pre-seed or seed stages but do not provide sufficient financing for start-ups to reach scale, particularly for digital start-ups that need capital to scale up quickly.

Box 6.2

Terminology in venture capital private equity markets

Venture capital financing rounds with a focus on digital entrepreneurship

Start-ups typically go through several growth stages during which they receive different types and amounts of financing. This box describes these stages and provides a map of financing instruments with the support of the World Bank.

Friends and family round. At the earliest stages, founders usually rely on funding from friends and family who are supportive and hardly ever conduct any due diligence on the aspiring company. Typically, friends and family investors would still receive convertible notes or a simple agreement for future equity (SAFE) for their investments but may also receive

common stock (see later in this box for definitions). The amounts raised lie between US$5,000 and US$200,000 at this stage and tend to be lower in developing economies (across all stages).

Seed stage (and pre-seed). At the seed stage, funding will usually come from people or organizations without close personal connection to the entrepreneur. Typically, investors at the seed stage are angel investors—affluent individuals who see the potential for a long-term return on an early investment and mostly also bring in their networks, expertise, and experience to support an early venture.[a] At this stage, the start-up entrepreneur will usually have put together a "pitch deck" to describe its business

continued

Box 6.2, *continued*

model and prospects to potential investors. Investors at seed stage typically receive a convertible note or a SAFE but may also receive basic preferred stock such as Series Seed Preferred Stock. Investments range from US$250,000 to US$1 million at this round.

Early stage. Venture capital (VC) funds start investing in a company at the early stage when valuations are still low but the company's prospects are clearer than in the previous two rounds. In addition to VC funds, there may also be angel investors investing at this stage. Both usually receive preferred stock such as Series Seed Preferred Stock but may also receive convertible notes (SAFEs are less common). Investments tend to range between US$500,000 and US$1 million in the early-stage round. However, it is not uncommon that companies move directly from seed stage to Series A.

Series A. With typical valuations over US$1 million, the Series A round of financing is the largest funding round a company will have had at this point and will also take the longest time to complete. Investors are predominantly VC funds that receive preferred stock connected to rights such as a seat on the company's board of directors and the right to participate in subsequent funding rounds.

Subsequent rounds. Companies that grow and scale up as hoped will continue with several rounds (Series B, C, D, E), each with higher valuations (ideally).

Mezzanine. Companies may use a mix of debt and equity financing—called a mezzanine round of financing—usually before an initial public offering and if investors do not wish for their investment to be diluted further by raising additional equity. Businesses usually issue subordinate debt or preferred equity (for example, using convertible notes) or a combination.

Types of securities instruments
Common stock. With common stock, investors receive a share of the company depending on their investment and the company valuation. Although this type of security is straightforward and easy for companies and investors to understand, it may not be ideal for any new company because it requires the company to be valuated, which may be particularly difficult for digital start-ups.

Preferred stock. Preferred stock in the VC context is equity shares with higher liquidation priority than common stock and also requires an estimate of the company's value. Professional VC investors tend to expect this type of security in exchange for their early financial support.

a. Angel investors usually have to demonstrate net worth or income thresholds required by the jurisdiction's securities laws to qualify as "accredited investors."

Private VC resources therefore provide critical funding that allows successful start-ups to expand.

Investments in start-ups at seed stage are deemed risky and too small in ticket size by private VC, leading to an undersupply of private funding. Although private VCs specialize in high-risk–high-return investments, they may be deterred by the high probability of a start-up's failure at early stages (that is, seed stage). There are several reasons why this shortage of VC funding is particularly challenging in developing economies (Divakaran, McGinnis, and Shariff 2014). First, investors usually have more opportunities to invest in larger and more established companies in developed economies that have lower risk profiles but struggle with access to finance. Second, the obstacles to investing in start-ups or SMEs in developing economies are greater because of perceived higher country and political risks, transaction costs, and information needs. Third, VC funds in developing economies lack a pool of talent capable of conducting valuation and underwriting of such investments. When no private VC market exists, either because of regulatory barriers or capital market development limitations, governments can consider providing government VC capital to crowd-in private investors to create a market (Fazekas and Becsky-Nagy 2021). See box 6.3.

Governments have a range of options with which to support the VC market, each with its own advantages and disadvantages and varying degrees of involvement. Depending on the constraints and dynamics of the VC market, the government may take a more active or passive supporting role. Table 6.2 provides a summary of government support mechanisms to VC markets.

Research suggests that the success of start-ups—for example, the likelihood of successful exits through initial public offerings or mergers and acquisitions—depends on the right amount of government involvement in VC investments (Brander, Du, and Hellmann 2010; see also Grilli and Murtinu 2012). In some countries, start-ups with some government-supported VC funding perform better than those with purely private investments.[2] However, if the government provides financing beyond what is needed to crowd-in private investors, weaker start-up performance results—pointing to a nonmonotonic relationship (Brander, Du, and Hellmann 2010). There is also evidence from emerging economies suggesting that best-performing high-growth start-ups dislike investors with government ties (Colonnelli, Li, and Liu 2023).

Box 6.3

Blended finance

Blended finance is an umbrella term that describes the strategic use of development finance for the mobilization of additional finance toward sustainable development in developing economies (OECD 2021). It usually relies on relatively small amounts of concessional donor funds to improve the risk-return profile for private investors and crowd-in their investments in support of projects in line with the Sustainable Development Goals. Blended finance solutions can involve debt, equity, risk-sharing, or guarantee products.

To enhance the use of blended finance instruments for private sector projects, the International Finance Corporation has developed five principles:

- *Rationale for blended concessional finance.* Contribution that is beyond what is available, otherwise absent from the market, and should not crowd out the private sector.
- *Crowding-in and minimum concessionality.* Contribute to catalyzing market development and mobilization of private sector resources, with concessionality not greater than necessary.
- *Commercial sustainability.* Impact achieved by each operation should aim to be sustainable and contribute to commercial viability.
- *Reinforcing markets.* Addresses market failures effectively and efficiently minimizes the risk of market distortion or crowding out of private finance.
- *Promoting high standards.* Promote adherence to high standards, including in areas of corporate governance, environmental impact, integrity, transparency, and disclosure.

Source: IFC 2021.

TABLE 6.2 Brief overview of government support mechanisms to the VC market

MECHANISM	DESCRIPTION	ROLE OF GOVERNMENT	ROLE OF PRIVATE INVESTORS (ESPECIALLY VC)
Government VC fund	Government sets up own VC fund and invests directly in companies.	Active investor; provides financing and makes investment decisions	Advises in investment decisions; makes follow-on investments
Co-investment fund	Government and private investors invest jointly (with varying degrees of decision-making power).	Active or passive investor	Active investor
Fund of funds	Government invests in private VC funds and only indirectly into companies.	Passive investor	Active investor (manages funds for the government)
Backstopping or loss and profit sharing	Government partially covers potential losses of private investors or shares profits.	Active or passive investor	Active investor
Credit guarantees and subsidized loans (in mezzanine finance)	Government backs lending to entrepreneurs to lower borrowing costs.	Guarantor	Lender; active investor
Capacity-building grants by governments to prepare start-ups for PE/VC investments	Governments provide funding to intermediary organizations to build the capacity of start-ups to be PE/VC-ready firms, for example, digital and business skills training, marketing, networking, business plan generation.	Sponsor	Cosponsor (given mutual interest)

Source: Original table for this publication.
Note: PE = private equity; VC = venture capital.

6.4 CONSULTATION AND VALIDATION EXERCISE WITH STAKEHOLDERS

At this stage of the analysis, stakeholders, including policy makers, entrepreneurs, and IOs, should be consulted about the findings of the assessment. The consultation exercise plays an important role from two perspectives. First, learning directly from stakeholders about information that is usually not captured by other data sources, such as administrative data and surveys, proposed across different modules, is crucial. Second, stakeholders should be involved as part of the process to validate the findings and build institutional support for the policy recommendations.

A qualitative method, such as a focus group questionnaire, can be used to gain a deeper understanding of the on-the-ground realities and challenges. This exercise can focus on three groups of stakeholders: policy makers, IOs (including accelerators, incubators, venture capitalists, mentors, universities, networking and information platforms, and financial and banking institutions), and firms and entrepreneurs (including early-stage entrepreneurs).

The focus group can cover five dimensions. These dimensions are based on the entrepreneurial ecosystem assessment conceptual framework described in the introduction to this toolkit. "Policy" refers to the adoption of good practices related to the design and implementation of policies to support entrepreneurship. "Governance and leadership" refer to the extent and quality of relationships (focusing on coordination and cooperation) between various stakeholders in the ecosystem.

- Endowment factors (physical capital and infrastructure, human capital, and knowledge)
- Demand for factors (market incentives, firm capabilities, entrepreneurial characteristics)

- Barriers (access to finance, regulations, culture, and social network)
- Policy design and implementation
- Governance and leadership.

An important step in this exercise is the identification of key players and the method for implementation. This toolkit provides a proposed questionnaire (online appendix E)[3] for conducting this exercise, based on the pilots in Kenya, Romania, and Central America.

6.5 PRIORITIZING ACTIONS AND PACKAGING ENTREPRENEURSHIP POLICY

Several steps should be followed to prioritize policy areas based on the ecosystem analysis:

Find existing gaps. These modules provide evidence on the existing gaps in the development of the private sector. These gaps can be classified as barriers to supply factors, to demand factors, or to the allocation of those resources to the firms. The results of those existing gaps will also show up as gaps in new firms' entry rates, their growth patterns, or the innovation cycle. In this step, the main objective is to have a comprehensive view of the opportunities and gaps in the ecosystem. The next steps will help prioritize and identify which gaps are the biggest constraints at the time of the analysis.

Identify binding constraints. Finding gaps in the ecosystem does not imply that an intervention should be designed or implemented. For example, finding that there is no VC does not imply that governments should subsidize the creation of a venture fund. The impact and relevance of such interventions will be determined by the stage of development of the ecosystem and an economic analysis of the binding constraints. A venture fund in an ecosystem without a good pipeline of high-potential entrepreneurs, or without a developed financial system that generates exit options for the fund, will not have any impact. Consequently, this second step aims to identify the binding constraints that can explain the existence of the gaps identified in step 1. The main inputs for this analysis will be the stage of development of the ecosystem, the conceptual framework from this toolkit, and the data collected from program managers. The expected outcome of this analysis would be to answer two questions: First, what is the main barrier for the ecosystem (such as a lack of new firm entry, low quality or low potential of existing firms, or lagging innovation processes to scale up)? Second, given that barrier, what are the binding constraints that have caused it?

Understand the market and policy failures. After identifying the binding constraints, it is important to understand the public sector's role when intervening in the market. Interventions are justified when market or policy failures exist. Beyond the typical market failures, some of the constraints may come from the nature of entrepreneurship itself. For example, new ventures will not have a track record to support their projections, or they may create new markets, implying that there are no suitable comparisons for valuing the firm. Other constraints can come from government regulations that discourage starting new firms or that limit the growth potential of existing ones. Importantly, the existence of a market failure does not mean that the government will have the capability to diagnose and improve the status quo in all circumstances. Hence, in this step policy makers need to ask two questions: First, what are the market or policy failures that need to be solved? Second, can a public intervention solve this failure? Table 6.1 and the conceptual framework can help policy makers answer these two questions by allowing them to understand why and how interventions can be designed to solve the binding constraints identified in step 2.

Consider existing policies and interventions. The fourth step is to map the existing policy and support landscape in the ecosystem. Module 4 provides a detailed discussion on the type of information that should be collected from both the public and private sector. The importance of these data in the prioritization of the policy mix is twofold. First, in many cases, it is more efficient to adjust and improve existing interventions that already have an infrastructure and that are part of the ecosystem than it is to start new actions that do not build on what is already available. Second, as described in the final step, the impact of an intervention will depend on the existing gaps and endowments in the ecosystem, along with the complementarities that it can generate.

Review intervention options. The next step is to learn from other policies and existing evidence on what does and does not work. Table 6.1 provides some success and failure factors for each area of intervention, as well as references to research on how policy makers can unbind some of the existing constraints.

Create the prioritization and action plan. Finally, with the list of available interventions, evidence, and a clear conceptual framework, the last step is to design a policy mix that fits the ecosystem's development stage and considers the complementarities of interventions and barriers. The interventions included in this policy mix need to complement each other so that an entrepreneur who solves one of the constraints does not immediately face another one. This integrated ecosystem approach—instead of specific, isolated firm-level interventions—could generate more positive agglomeration externalities that overcome congestion costs.

Proposed interventions can be sequenced by time, impact, resource, and cost considerations. The key challenges to implementing the proposed interventions should be highlighted, along with the proposed timeline for implementation. These can, for example, be split between the short term (within two years), medium term (two to five years), and long term (five or more years). Particular attention should be given to "quick wins," which are visible, have immediate benefit, and can be delivered quickly.

The results of the policy analysis can be expressed as a matrix that identifies priorities for the ecosystem, time frames, and quick wins that help push the agenda as a whole. One example, based on the diagnostics for Romania, could be to classify policies as either mission critical, flagship, or foundational long term (table 6.3). *Mission critical* refers to activities that are extremely time sensitive, for example, because the government is currently designing the new policies or laying the groundwork for future recommendations. *Flagship* refers to crucial activities that should be undertaken to further develop the entrepreneurial ecosystem. *Foundational long term* refers to crucial activities that require a longer time horizon to come to fruition because other "foundational" elements need to be sequenced and prioritized first. Table 6.3 provides an example of a policy mix created using this approach in Romania. Each policy recommendation comes from the results of the diagnostic phase, combined with the conceptual framework and the existing evidence on best practices.

Finally, it is critical to implement a robust monitoring and evaluation (M&E) system. Evidence across countries, including data collected over the pilots for this toolkit, suggests that this is rare. Among the few programs and IOs

TABLE 6.3 **Example of policy mix following the entrepreneurship toolkit**

POLICY RECOMMENDATIONS	PRIORITIZATION	TIME SENSITIVE	QUICK WIN
Recalibrate the policy mix for starting and scaling high-quality innovative firms by (1) improving the functionality of instruments, and (2) implementing a comprehensive package of reforms tailored to high-quality innovative firms.	Mission critical	Yes	Yes
Reform regulations to strengthen entrepreneurship and investments.	Mission critical	Yes	Yes
Establish a one-stop agency "ecosystem hub."	Mission critical	Yes	Yes
Strengthen ecosystem enablers.	Flagship	Yes	
Create a start-up fund.	Flagship		
Improve entrepreneurship education and strengthen the role of universities in the ecosystem.	Flagship	Yes	
Implement start-up visa program.	Flagship	Yes	Yes
Build and promote a network of Romanian founders and diaspora.	Flagship		
Scale up through exports.	Flagship		
Foster knowledge spillovers into the private sector.	Foundational long term	Yes	
Promote the digital economy.	Foundational long term	Yes	

Source: Cruz et al. 2022.
Note: Mission critical = activities that are extremely time sensitive; *flagship* = crucial activities that should be undertaken to further develop the entrepreneurial ecosystem; *foundational long term* = crucial activities that require a longer time horizon to come to fruition.

conducting M&E systems, only a very small share have counterfactual analysis aiming to understand the impact of these interventions. Further discussion about the importance of these exercises, including description of methods and detailed examples in practice, is provided in Gertler et al. (2016).

6.6 HOW THE WORLD BANK CAN SUPPORT ENTREPRENEURIAL ECOSYSTEMS

The World Bank can support entrepreneurial ecosystem policy using its full range of lending products. Considering the total number of lending operations during the fiscal years of 2015–21, including Investment Project Financing (IPF) projects, Development Policy Financing (DPF) projects, and Program-for-Results Financing, the number of approved (International Bank for Reconstruction and Development) entrepreneurship-supporting projects has been steadily increasing, from two projects (or 0.6 percent of projects) in 2015 to 42 (or 11.4 percent) in 2021 (figure 6.1).[4] The Finance, Competitiveness, and Innovation (FCI) Global Practice leads among World Bank Global Practices in lending operations focused on entrepreneurship. Over this period, 44 such projects were undertaken by FCI, followed by the Agriculture Global Practice with 15 projects and the Social Protection and Jobs Global Practice with 10. Total lending projects supporting some entrepreneurship activity

FIGURE 6.1

World Bank operations supporting entrepreneurship

a. Number of lending projects

b. Share of projects and commitments

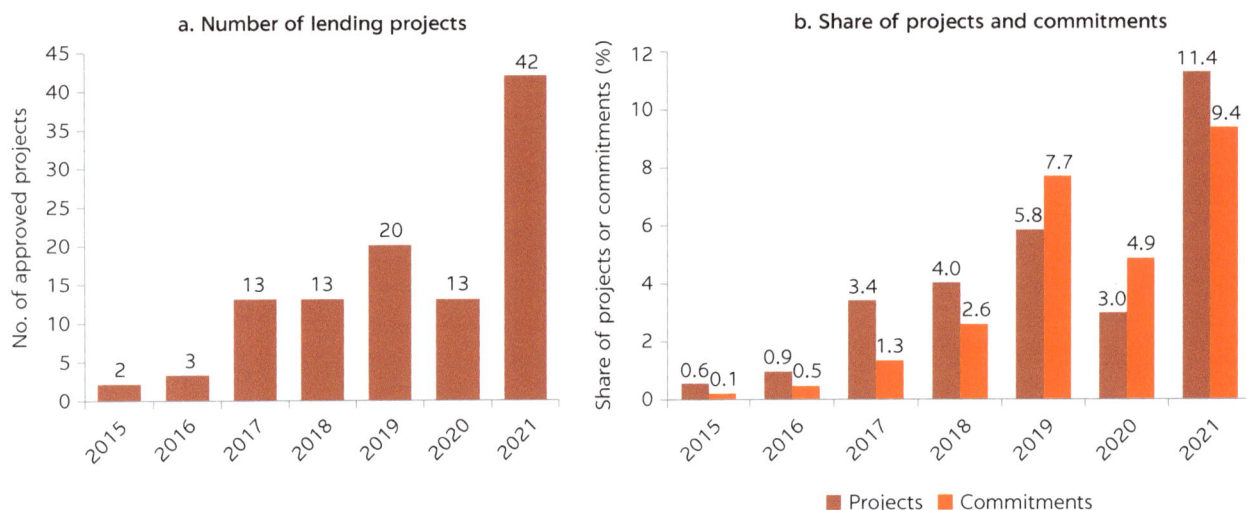

Source: Original figure for this publication.
Note: Results based on all active and closed lending projects that were approved in FY2015–21. Includes all International Bank for Reconstruction and Development / International Development Association projects that list "entrepreneurship" as a theme, or "entrepreneurship" appears in the project's development objectives or in one of its components.

amounted to more than US$5 billion in 2021 and has been increasing over time, with large numbers of projects concentrated in Africa and the Middle East and North Africa region.

In addition to financial instruments funding public policies, the World Bank also supports the development of entrepreneurial ecosystems through the International Finance Corporation (IFC), the private sector arm of the World Bank. The IFC has been expanding its support to tech ecosystems with a new VC platform that is expected to invest up to US$225 million in start-ups across Africa, the Middle East, Central Asia, and Pakistan. Moreover, the IFC has been investing in seed funds, accelerators, and incubators in emerging markets that are helping early-stage companies grow and become ready for later-stage investment.

A single instrument on its own is unlikely to transform entrepreneurial ecosystems, given the multitude of challenges that countries face. Because of the complex and connected nature of ecosystem challenges, policy mixes that use a variety of instruments targeting different elements within a single operation can be found in many World Bank projects. Particular focus should be given to policy mixes likely to exhibit synergies, such as combining capacity building with access to finance, thereby maximizing the effect of the additional financing. However, the optimal policy mixes in practice will depend largely on the specific conditions of each country and beneficiary group (World Bank Group 2021).

IPF can be used to support entrepreneurial ecosystems across all ecosystem pillars. Table 6.4 lists common examples of IPF entrepreneurship projects across the policy areas they support along with their policy instruments.[5] However, other types of projects with broader goals may also indirectly support entrepreneurial ecosystems, such as the building of roads or improving education. Further, at times the same project or policy instrument can serve multiple policy areas. For example, matching grants targeted at exporters may improve both access to finance and access to markets, with the former enabling the latter.

TABLE 6.4 **Examples of common IPF projects to support entrepreneurial ecosystems**

POLICY AREA	POLICY INSTRUMENTS (EXAMPLES)	IPF PROJECT EXAMPLE(S)
Physical capital and infrastructure	• Supporting incubators and accelerators and attracting global accelerators • Development of business parks • Special economic zone support • Support for special infrastructure	Bangladesh (P156113) Congo, Dem. Rep. (P160806) Ghana (P166539) Kenya (P161317)
Human capital	Tailored training and mentoring	Congo, Dem. Rep. (P160806) Egypt, Arab Rep. (P162835)
Knowledge capital	• Creating a start-up-university platform • Supporting incubators' and accelerators' capacity and quality • Connecting large companies and start-ups	Kenya (P161317)
Access to finance	• Small grants • Matching grants • Early-stage risk finance • Scale-up of capital through co-investment funds • Targeted debt financing • Support to nonbank finance organizations • Sequential finance instruments for different stages of firm development • Capacity building in financial institutions	Argentina (P159515) Congo, Dem. Rep. (P160806) Egypt, Arab Rep. (P162835) Ethiopia (P171034) Ghana (P166539) Jamaica (P152307) Morocco (P150928) Senegal (P146469)
Regulations	• Business regulation reform in general and along the firm life cycle • Capacity building SME agency support • Development of one-stop shops to streamline government services • Rationalization of support agencies • Reinforcement of institutions and systems to improve the business environment • Online publication of business regulations	Congo, Dem. Rep. (P160806) Congo, Rep. (P161590) Ghana (P166539) Mozambique (P173450) Senegal (P146469)
Social capital and culture	• Support for networks and links building connections • SME regulatory reform to reduce bias against women • Public awareness campaign on gender issues, especially women entrepreneurs	Congo, Dem. Rep. (P160806) Kenya (P161317)
Access to markets	• Build connections between entrepreneurs and markets • Connect large companies and start-ups • Competitions and matching grants to new exporters or firms with export potential • Export promotion and support • NQI reform • Supply chain finance • Supplier development • Export finance	Ethiopia (P171034) Ghana (P166539) Kenya (P161317) Moldova (P144103) Senegal (P146469) Tunisia (P132381)
Firm capabilities	• Tailored training, mentoring, coaching, advisory support • Capacity building to business development service providers and public SME agencies to improve services to entrepreneurs • NQI reform • Technology extension services	Congo, Dem. Rep. (P160806) Egypt, Arab Rep. (P162835) Ghana (P166539) Mozambique (P173450)
Entrepreneurial characteristics	• Business plan competitions • Training • Mentoring	Congo, Dem. Rep. (P160806) Egypt, Arab Rep. (P162835) Senegal (P146469)

Source: Original table for this publication.
Note: For more details on specific projects, visit the World Bank website (https://www.worldbank.org/en/home) and search on the P (project) number. IPF = Investment Project Financing; NQI = national quality infrastructure; SMEs = small and medium enterprises.

TABLE 6.5 **Examples of common DPF projects to support entrepreneurial ecosystems**

POLICY AREA	PRIOR ACTIONS (EXAMPLES)	DPF PROJECT EXAMPLE(S)
Physical capital and infrastructure	To promote the pooling of very high-speed networks and access to broadband connectivity, the borrower has taken the necessary measures for mutualized infrastructure deployments. To increase access to broadband, adopted resolutions and approved a list of eligible underserved areas.	Morocco (P174004)
Human capital	Removed two requirements to employ expatriate workers for a number of positions and extended the list of occupations eligible for work permits to facilitate a supply of high-skilled professionals. Approved the framework to identify groups lacking financial literacy. Increased university open enrollment while providing a course module on foreign languages and computer literacy. Broadened vocational training.	Indonesia (P172439) Morocco (P120566) Nepal (P173044) Tuvalu (P150194)
Knowledge capital	Created entrepreneurship-enhancing programs in the education system. Launched the accelerator program. Approved framework to guarantee university quality. Provided resources to state universities for institutional strengthening, research and innovation, teacher development, and outreach.	Chile (P154213) Ecuador (P171190) Mexico (P098299) Peru (P156858)
Access to finance	Adopted the draft law on microcredit and expanding microinsurance. Adopted the initial bylaws and share capital of the National Company for Guarantees. Proposed certain amendments for independence of the Insurance Commission. Approved the Credit Information Act, credit reporting unit, and the Credit Risk Database. Approved the amendments to the Secured Transactions Act, and to achieve interoperability for payment transactions, ban exclusivity arrangements, and rationalize customer fees. Issued a regulation to establish the Catastrophe Insurance Facility. Revised the investment directive for more diverse investment options. Issued a regulation on the establishment of digital banks. Notified the emergency credit line facility. Approved regulations on seed capital, venture capital, hedge funds, and private equity investors.	India (P174292) Morocco (P174004) Nepal (P173044) Philippines (P175008, P179361) Tunisia (P158111)
Regulations	To promote the development of start-ups and MSMEs, adopted the draft law. Adopted the law offering a more flexible legal framework for start-ups and simplified start-up requirements for low-risk businesses. Reduced the number of business activities subject to at least one investment restriction. Simplified import approval processes and waived all technical requirements for certain imports under certain conditions. Reduced compliance costs by removing compulsory certification for steel, stove, and wire products used by producers. Adopted law streamlining investment entry authorizations. Simplified bankruptcy regime. Amendments to improve labor market flexibility.	Botswana (P175934) India (P174292) Indonesia (P172439) Morocco (P174004) Nepal (P173044) Pakistan (P090690) Philippines (P179361) Tunisia (P158111)

continued

TABLE 6.5, *continued*

POLICY AREA	PRIOR ACTIONS (EXAMPLES)	DPF PROJECT EXAMPLE(S)
Social capital and culture	Adopted and transmitted to parliament the draft law to establish measures supporting the share of women on boards of directors.	Argentina (P083982)
		Morocco (P174004)
	Promoted links between large firms and SMEs and among SMEs through two new programs.	Nepal (P173044)
Access to markets	Adopted a decree to make the public procurement portal mandatory, to improve SME access to public procurement.	Colombia (P173424)
		Morocco (P174004)
	Streamlined the processing of export transactions through the mandated use of online platforms.	Philippines (P170914)
	Updated the national logistics policy.	
Firm capabilities	Adopted criteria to support implementation of a mobile money system.	Egypt, Arab Rep. (P168630)
		Georgia (P149998)
	Approved the retail payments strategy aimed at the development of digital payment services.	Nepal (P173044)
		Philippines (P179361)
	Approved the framework that identifies key target groups lacking financial literacy.	Vietnam (P176717)
	Issued decree providing technical assistance for entrepreneurs.	
	Established the Entrepreneurship Development Agency.	
Entrepreneurial characteristics	Issued a circular to provide training with targeted interventions to women.	Nepal (P173044)

Source: World Bank operations portal.
Note: These are examples of prior actions and projects associated with them. Prior actions have been edited for clarity and brevity. DPF = Development Policy Financing; MSMEs = micro, small, and medium enterprises; SMEs = small and medium enterprises.

DPF can support and enable the conditions for improving entrepreneurial ecosystem pillars through reforms. Table 6.5 lists common examples of DPF projects with entrepreneurship implications across the policy areas they support along with their prior actions.[6] However, other types of DPF projects with broader goals, such as telecom or energy reforms, may also indirectly support entrepreneurial ecosystems. By their nature, DPF projects tend to focus on regulatory improvements, which most often affect the barriers to accumulation for demand and supply factors, but they can also improve other ecosystem pillars. These examples may provide suggestions to task-team leaders on interventions and regulatory reforms that may open further opportunities for mobilizing further private sector investment.

More detailed guidance for World Bank lending operations on various specific aspects of the entrepreneurial ecosystem is also available across several toolkits and notes. For example, "Strengthening World Bank SME-Support Interventions: Operational Guidance Document" (World Bank Group 2021) presents practical advice for World Bank operations, parts of which apply to the entrepreneurial ecosystem as well. Similarly, for interventions related to innovation, crucial information can be found in Cirera et al. (2020). An overview of the many relevant guidance notes for lending operations can also be found in World Bank Group (2021). Nedayvoda et al. (2021) provide a broader perspective of instruments and stages of financing deep tech companies. Figure 6.2 shows a World Bank Group approach to pulling together different financial instruments to provide funding for digital start-ups, leveraging comparative advantages of public funding and private investors, highlighting the complementarity across instruments led by the World Bank (International Bank for Reconstruction and Development and International Development Association) and the IFC along the life cycle of the firm. Table 6.6 provides further details on mapping the start-up financing instruments within the World Bank.

FIGURE 6.2

Summary of World Bank Group Maximizing Finance for Development approach to funding digital start-ups

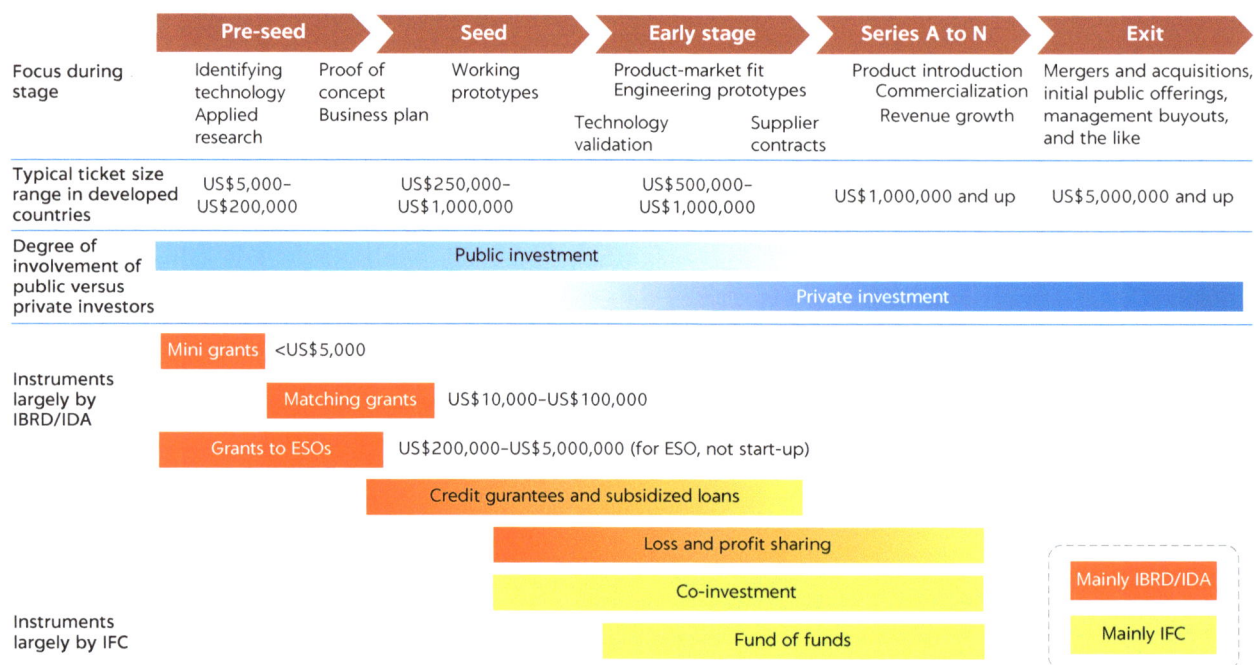

Sources: Based on Fazekas and Becsky-Nagy 2021; Nedayvoda et al. 2021; and World Bank project appraisal documents.
Note: ESO = entrepreneurship support organization; IBRD = International Bank for Reconstruction and Development; IDA = International Development Association; IFC = International Finance Corporation.

TABLE 6.6 **Mapping of start-up financing instruments within the World Bank (beyond VC markets)**

FINANCING INSTRUMENT	TARGET STAGES AND TYPICAL TICKET SIZE	DESCRIPTION AND OBJECTIVE	RESPONSIBLE INSTITUTIONS	MARKET OR GOVERNMENT FAILURES BEING ADDRESSED	IMPLEMENTATION RISKS
Mini grants (similar terms: cash grants, formalization grants)	Pre-seed <US$5,000	Small grants to support entrepreneurs at pre-investment and pre-creation stages, for example, for business formalization or development of business plans. Low level of safeguards and reporting requirements. Aims to increase idea generation of disadvantaged entrepreneurs, foster entrepreneurial mindsets of youth (for example, idea competitions).	IBRD, IDA Disbursement through government agencies, IOs	Mini grant recipients often cannot access commercial loans (for example, because of lack of collateral or income).	Early businesses founded with mini grants are not yet viable investments for VC investors.

continued

TABLE 6.6, *continued*

FINANCING INSTRUMENT	TARGET STAGES AND TYPICAL TICKET SIZE	DESCRIPTION AND OBJECTIVE	RESPONSIBLE INSTITUTIONS	MARKET OR GOVERNMENT FAILURES BEING ADDRESSED	IMPLEMENTATION RISKS
Matching grants (similar term: co-investment grants)	Pre-seed and seed US$5k–US$100k	Grants to young and small private enterprises to stimulate the development of innovative start-ups (grants are usually not given to individuals). Public funding tied to contribution from private sector organizations (usually between 10 and 50 percent). Grant recipients need to comply with reporting requirements for social and environmental safeguards.	IBRD, IDA Disbursement through government agencies, IOs	Crowd-in private investors who are otherwise deterred by an unattractive risk-return profile of early ventures. Involvement of private sector investors to ensure selection of businesses on grounds of commercial viability rather than political favoritism. Increase exposure of entrepreneurs to private investor expertise and networks.	Reporting requirements on safeguards increase with grant size. Matching grants above US$100k tend to become too bureaucratic, while risks of misallocation of public funds increase. Grant sizes may not be large enough to generate VC investment-ready start-ups.
Grants and capacity building subsidies to IOs	Pre-seed and seed US$200k–US$2m (per ESO, not start-up)	Financial support to private IOs (for example, accelerators, incubators, innovation hubs) to establish, upgrade, equip, or maintain their services. Funding may be tied to the responsibility of the ESO to conduct training for entrepreneurs, to provide networking and matchmaking activities with investors, or host innovation competitions. Technical assistance and training for IOs to improve their capacity to support entrepreneurs. For example, tracking the pipeline of entrepreneurs, increases attractiveness of start-ups for investors, approaches to investment facilitation (for example, identifying investors, matchmaking), assessing business models and markets.	IBRD, IDA Disbursement through government agencies, WB Training to IOs by external consultants (local or international)	Today's IOs are typically operated as private companies, but in developing countries with underdeveloped entrepreneurship ecosystems there may not be a viable business model for IOs to operate sustainably and they thus require public sector support. Capacity building to IOs addresses lack of entrepreneurial experience in developing countries and limited exposure to international investor networks.	Supporting IOs only provides indirect support to start-ups, and the program quality of IOs is critical. IOs are only one part of a larger entrepreneurial ecosystem that also includes the regulatory framework, infrastructure, and skills. Grants may not be sufficient for IOs to become financially sustainable organizations that last without further financial support (that is, limited sustainability).
Co-investment VC	Early stage to later stage (series) US$500k and up	Public investment in private companies alongside private investors (that is, usually equity investments, not debt or grant). Role of government may be either active or passive (or mix) regarding selection of start-ups, depending on whether there are social and public policy objectives in eligibility criteria. Best practice is to let private investors drive the decision to ensure commercial principles are reflected and the public investments better utilized.	IBRD, IDA to set up public investments that match private investor (usually 20–50 percent, sometimes up to 80 percent if private market is too small). IFC (for example, through parts of the SME Ventures program, or Startup Catalyst).	Directly lowers the risk for private investors due to involvement of public investments, which usually assumes a lower liquidation preference. The public investment may therefore bridge a financing gap between seed and early stage and offer graduation pathways for digital entrepreneurs.	The implementation of co-investment schemes crucially depends on the specifics of the arrangement between private and public investors; for example, regarding liquidation preferencing in case of exits, specifics of government involvement in selection of investment projects, and definition of thresholds for public investments.

continued

TABLE 6.6, *continued*

FINANCING INSTRUMENT	TARGET STAGES AND TYPICAL TICKET SIZE	DESCRIPTION AND OBJECTIVE	RESPONSIBLE INSTITUTIONS	MARKET OR GOVERNMENT FAILURES BEING ADDRESSED	IMPLEMENTATION RISKS
Fund of funds	Early stage to later stage (series) US$500k and up	Investment of government or development banks in a portfolio of private VC funds to increase overall volume of VC financing. Typically, the fund of funds approach sets an upper limit on the amount of public investment into each VC fund (for example, 25 percent). Public investments in private VC funds include debt, quasi-equity, and equity and are usually tied to public objectives (for example, sectoral focus such as GreenTech).	IFC (for example, through parts of the SME Ventures program, or the IFC Global Emerging Markets Fund of Funds) IBRD, IDA—loans and grants to funds might complement IFC to further increase volume if the private market is too small.	Addresses underdeveloped VC financing ecosystem.	Although the fund of funds approach increases the volume of VC funding available in a market or sector, it does not necessarily alter the risk-return profile for investments in individual start-ups. Regulations and legal obstacles might limit the likelihood of the adoption of the fund of funds approach in less developed capital markets.
Loss and profit sharing (similar terms: backstopping, first-loss arrangements)	Early stage to later stage (series) US$500k and up but with a maximum limit on ticket size that can receive subsidies	Protecting a VC fund against losses by covering losses (or those above a certain limit) through public funding. A similar approach is that the public investor only gets a disproportionately smaller share of its profits, thereby raising the returns for the private sector.	IDA, IBRD IFC For example, IDA or IBRD can engage in first loss, then IFC as second loss, and so on.	The loss and profit-sharing instrument lowers the collateral requirements for loans to SMEs or start-ups for participating financial institutions. This allows them to increase lending to or investment in emerging ventures.	Loss and profit sharing may lead to private investors lowering their due diligence for investments given that they carry only a part of the risk (that is, moral hazard).
Credit guarantees (similar term: loan guarantees)	Early stage to later stage (series) US$500k and up but with a maximum limit on ticket size that can receive subsidies	Governments or development banks may also issue credit guarantees for financial institutions that lend to start-ups or SMEs to carry the risk of default.	IDA, IBRD IFC	Allows financial institutions to increase lending to start-ups with a high risk of default.	The instrument relies on a realistic estimate of default risks of start-ups given that this determines the amount of public money required for it. In the past, the default risk has tended to be underestimated (see, for example, the case of France in Lerner [2012]).
Subsidized loans	Early stage to later stage (series) US$500k–US$5m	Governments provide subsidized loans to entrepreneurs who would not be able to afford loans at market rates. Loans are commonly administered by private financial institutions. Approaches may involve setting lending requirements (for example, interest rates) for certain credit lines, refinancing schemes (that is, banks can borrow funds for earmarked purposes), or interest rate subsidies.	IDA, IBRD	Allows companies to borrow at below-market rates and thereby strengthen their access to finance.	Subsidized loans only address the cost of borrowing but not necessarily problems related to the lack of collateral or credit history that prevent entrepreneurs from accessing finance. Private banks may raise interest rates on other nonsubsidized credit lines to cross-finance the more favorable credits (Ornelas et al. 2019).

Source: World Bank, based on Colombo, Cumming, and Vismara 2016; Divakaran, McGinnis, and Shariff 2014; Fazekas and Becsky-Nagy 2021; Lerner, Leamon, and Garcia-Robles 2020; and World Bank project appraisal documents.

Note: ESO = entrepreneurship support organization; IBRD = International Bank for Reconstruction and Development; IDA = International Development Association; IFC = International Finance Corporation; IOs = intermediary organizations supporting entrepreneurship; k = thousand; m = million; SME = small and medium enterprise; VC = venture capital; WB = World Bank.

NOTES

1. Please also refer to "Advancing SMEs' Growth and Productivity towards Better Government Support in SME Access to Finance" (World Bank, forthcoming) for guidance in designing such funding facilities in World Bank projects.
2. For a discussion of empirical evidence on government-supported venture capital, see Cirera et al. (2020).
3. Online appendixes A through F are available at https://openknowledge.worldbank.org /handle/10986/40305.
4. Entrepreneurship projects here include all projects where "entrepreneurship" is listed as a theme or appears in the project's development objectives or as a component. However, entrepreneurial ecosystem support can be even broader.
5. This list of examples is not exhaustive.
6. This list of examples is not exhaustive.

REFERENCES

Akcigit, Ufuk, John Grigsby, Tom Nicholas, and Stefanie Stantcheva. 2018. "Taxation and Innovation in the 20th Century." Working Paper 24982, National Bureau of Economic Research, Cambridge, MA. https://doi.org/10.3386/w24982.

Alaref, Jumana, Stefanie Brodmann, and Patrick Premand. 2020. "The Medium-Term Impact of Entrepreneurship Education on Labor Market Outcomes: Experimental Evidence from University Graduates in Tunisia." *Labour Economics* 62 (January): 101787. https://doi .org/10.1016/j.labeco.2019.101787.

Anderson, Stephen J., and David McKenzie. 2021. "What Prevents More Small Firms from Using Professional Business Services? An Information and Quality-Rating Experiment in Nigeria." Policy Research Working Paper 9614, World Bank, Washington, DC. https://doi .org/10.1596/1813-9450-9614.

Anderson, Stephen J., and David McKenzie. 2022. "Improving Business Practices and the Boundary of the Entrepreneur: A Randomized Experiment Comparing Training, Consulting, Insourcing, and Outsourcing." *Journal of Political Economy* 130 (1): 157–209. https://doi .org/10.1086/717044.

Assinova, V. 2020. "Early-Stage Venture Incubation and Mentoring Promote Learning, Scaling, and Profitability among Disadvantaged Entrepreneurs." *Organization Science* 31 (6): 1560–78.

Barsoum, Ghada, Bruno Crépon, Drew Gardiner, Bastien Michel, and William Parienté. 2022. "Evaluating the Impact of Entrepreneurship Edutainment in Egypt: An Experimental Approach." *Economica* 89 (353): 82–109.

Biancalani, Francesco, Dirk Czarnitzki, and Massimo Riccaboni. 2022. "The Italian Start Up Act: A Microeconometric Program Evaluation." *Small Business Economics* 58 (3): 1699–720. https://doi.org/10.1007/s11187-021-00468-7.

Bjorvatn, Kjetil, Alexander W. Cappelen, Linda Helgesson Sekei, Erik Ø. Sørensen, and Bertil Tungodden. 2020. "Teaching through Television: Experimental Evidence on Entrepreneurship Education in Tanzania." *Management Science* 66 (6): 2308–25. https://doi .org/10.1287/mnsc.2019.3321.

Brander, James A., Qianqian Du, and Thomas F. Hellmann. 2010. "The Effects of Government-Sponsored Venture Capital: International Evidence." Working Paper 16521, National Bureau of Economic Research, Cambridge, MA. https://doi.org/10.3386/w16521.

Cai, Jing, and Adam Szeidl. 2018. "Interfirm Relationships and Business Performance." *Quarterly Journal of Economics* 133 (3): 1229–82. https://doi.org/10.1093/qje/qjx049.

Chatterji, S. 2019. "Market Power and Spatial Competition in Rural India." Cambridge Working Papers in Economics 1921, Faculty of Economics, University of Cambridge, Cambridge, UK.

Chioda, Laura, David Contreras-Loya, Paul Gertler, and Dana Carney. 2021. "Making Entrepreneurs: Returns to Training Youth in Hard Versus Soft Business Skills." Working Paper 28845, National Bureau of Economic Research, Cambridge, MA. https://doi .org/10.3386/w28845.

Cho, Yoonyoung, and Maddalena Honorati. 2014. "Entrepreneurship Programs in Developing Countries: A Meta Regression Analysis." *Labour Economics* 28 (June): 110–30. https://doi .org/10.1016/j.labeco.2014.03.011.

Cirera, X., D. Comin, and M. Cruz. 2022. *Bridging the Technological Divide: Technology Adoption by Firms in Developing Countries.* Washington, DC: World Bank.

Cirera, X., J. Frias, J. Hill, and Y. Li. 2020. *A Practitioner's Guide to Innovation Policy: Instruments to Build Firm Capabilities and Accelerate Technological Catch-Up in Developing Countries.* Washington, DC: World Bank.

Colombo, Massimo G., Douglas J. Cumming, and Silvio Vismara. 2016. "Governmental Venture Capital for Innovative Young Firms." *Journal of Technology Transfer* 41: 10–24.

Colonnelli, Emanuele, Bo Li, and Ernest Liu. Forthcoming. "Investing with the Government: A Field Experiment in China." *Journal of Political Economy.* https://doi.org/10.1086 /726237.

Cornelli, Giulio, Sebastian Doerr, Lavinia Franco, and Jon Frost. 2021. "Funding for Fintechs: Patterns and Drivers." *BIS Quarterly Review* Special Feature (September). https://www.bis .org/publ/qtrpdf/r_qt2109c.htm.

Cornelli, Giulio, Jon Frost, Leonardo Gambacorta, P. Raghavendra Rau, Robert Wardrop, and Tania Ziegler. 2020. "Fintech and Big Tech Credit: A New Database." Working Paper 887, Bank for International Settlements, Basel. https://www.bis.org/publ/work887.pdf.

Cruz, Marcio, Natasha Kapil, Pablo Andres Astudillo Estevez, Christopher David Haley, Zoe Cordelia Lu, and Pelin Arslan. 2022. *Starting Up Romania: Entrepreneurship Ecosystem Diagnostic.* Washington, DC: World Bank Group. http://documents.worldbank.org/curated /en/099920106072238493/P174325083a5cc0eb090350dcde4c6a32df.

Cruz, Marcio, Daniel Lederman, and Laura Zoratto. 2018. "The Anatomy and the Impact of Export Promotion Agencies." In *Research Handbook on Economic Diplomacy*, by Peter A. G. van Bergeijk and Selwin J. V. Moons, 94–108. Cheltenham, Gloucester, UK: Edward Elgar Publishing.

Da Rin, Marco, Marina Di Giacomo, and Alessandro Sembenelli. 2011. "Entrepreneurship, Firm Entry, and the Taxation of Corporate Income: Evidence from Europe." In "The Role of Firms in Tax Systems," special issue, *Journal of Public Economics* 95 (9): 1048–66. https://doi .org/10.1016/j.jpubeco.2010.06.010.

De Mel, Suresh, David McKenzie, and Christopher Woodruff. 2008. "Returns to Capital in Microenterprises: Evidence from a Field Experiment." *Quarterly Journal of Economics* 123 (4): 1329–72.

Didier, Tatiana, and Beulah Chelva. 2022. Private Equity Markets in EMDEs. Washington, DC: World Bank.

Divakaran, Shanthi, Patrick J. McGinnis, and Masood Shariff. 2014. "Private Equity and Venture Capital in SMEs in Developing Countries: The Role for Technical Assistance." Policy Research Working Paper 6827, World Bank, Washington, DC. https://doi.org/10.1596 /1813-9450-6827.

Ezell, Stephen J., and Robert D. Atkinson. 2011. "International Benchmarking of Countries' Policies and Programs Supporting SME Manufacturers." Information Technology and Innovation Foundation, Washington, DC.

Fazekas, Balázs, and Patrícia Becsky-Nagy. 2021. "A New Theoretical Model of Government Backed Venture Capital Funding." *Acta Oeconomica* 71 (3): 487–506. https://doi .org/10.1556/032.2021.00024.

Frese, Michael, Michael M. Gielnik, and Mona Mensmann. 2016. "Psychological Training for Entrepreneurs to Take Action: Contributing to Poverty Reduction in Developing Countries." *Current Directions in Psychological Science* 25 (3): 196–202. https://doi.org/10.1177 /0963721416636957.

Gardner, C., and P. B. Henry. Forthcoming. "The Global Infrastructure Gap: Potential, Perils, and a Framework for Distinction." *Journal of Economic Literature.*

Gentry, William M., and R. Glenn Hubbard. 2000. "Tax Policy and Entrepreneurial Entry." *American Economic Review* 90 (2): 283–87. https://doi.org/10.1257/aer.90.2.283.

Gertler, Paul J., Sebastian Martinez, Patrick Premand, Laura B. Rawlings, and Christel M. J. Vermeersch. 2016. *Impact Evaluation in Practice, Second Edition*. Washington, DC: Inter-American Development Bank and World Bank.

Goñi, E., and S. Reyes. 2019. "On the Role of Resource Reallocation and Growth Acceleration of Productive Public Programs: Effectiveness of a Peruvian Dynamic Entrepreneurship Program and the Implications of Participants' Selection." Discussion Paper 707, Inter-American Development Bank, Washington, DC.

Gonzalez-Uribe, Juanita, and Michael Leatherbee. 2018. "The Effects of Business Accelerators on Venture Performance: Evidence from Start-Up Chile." *Review of Financial Studies* 31 (4): 1566–603. https://doi.org/10.1093/rfs/hhx103.

Gonzalez-Uribe, Juanita, and S. Reyes. 2021. "Identifying and Boosting 'Gazelles': Evidence from Business Accelerators." *Journal of Financial Economics* 139 (1): 260–87.

Grilli, Luca, and Samuele Murtinu. 2012. "Do Public Subsidies Affect the Performance of New Technology-Based Firms? The Importance of Evaluation Schemes and Agency Goals." *Prometheus* 30 (1): 97–111. https://doi.org/10.1080/08109028.2012.676836.

Grover, Arti, Somik V. Lall, and William F. Maloney. 2022. *Place, Productivity, and Prosperity*. Washington, DC: World Bank. https://doi.org/10.1596/978-1-4648-1670-3.

Guerzoni, Marco, Consuelo R. Nava, and Massimiliano Nuccio. 2021. "Start-Ups Survival through a Crisis: Combining Machine Learning with Econometrics to Measure Innovation." *Economics of Innovation and New Technology* 30 (5): 468–93. https://doi.org/10.1080/10438599.2020.1769810.

Gusberti, T. D. H., V. Ludvig, B. Wolff, G. Zuanazzi, and A. Peretti. 2017. "Business Intelligence and Technology Productization for Market for Technology, Idea and Knowledge." Conference Paper for R&D Management Conference, "Science, Markets, and Society: Crossing Boundaries Creating Momentum." Leuven, July 1–5.

Hjort, J., and J. Poulsen. 2019. "The Arrival of Fast Internet and Employment in Africa." *American Economic Review* 109 (3): 1032–79.

Iacovone, Leonardo, William Maloney, and David McKenzie. 2019. "Improving Management in Colombian Firms through Individual and Group Consulting." Finance and PSD Impact No. 53, World Bank, Washington, DC. https://openknowledge.worldbank.org/handle/10986/31843.

IFC (International Finance Corporation). 2021. "Using Blended Concessional Finance to Invest in Challenging Markets: Economic Considerations, Transparency, Governance, and Lessons of Experience." International Finance Corporation, Washington, DC. https://www.ifc.org/en/types/insights-reports/2021/using-blended-concessional-finance-to-invest-in-challenging-markets.

Kenney, Martin, Silvia Massini, and Thomas P. Murtha. 2009. "Introduction: Offshoring Administrative and Technical Work: New Fields for Understanding the Global Enterprise." *Journal of International Business Studies* 40 (6): 887–900. https://doi.org/10.1057/jibs.2009.22.

Lerner, Josh. 2012. *Boulevard of Broken Dreams: Why Public Efforts to Boost Entrepreneurship and Venture Capital Have Failed—and What to Do about It*. Princeton, NJ: Princeton University Press.

Lerner, Josh, Ann Leamon, and Susan Garcia-Robles. 2020. *Best Practices in Creating a Venture Capital Ecosystem*. Washington, DC: Multilateral Investment Fund.

McKenzie, David, and Christopher Woodruff. 2008. "Experimental Evidence on Returns to Capital and Access to Finance in Mexico." *World Bank Economic Review* 22 (3): 457–82. https://doi.org/10.1093/wber/lhn017.

McKenzie, David, and Christopher Woodruff. 2014. "What Are We Learning from Business Training and Entrepreneurship Evaluations around the Developing World?" *World Bank Research Observer* 29 (1): 48–82. https://doi.org/10.1093/wbro/lkt007.

McKenzie, David, Nabila Assaf, and Ana Paula Cusolito. 2017. "The Additionality Impact of a Matching Grant Programme for Small Firms: Experimental Evidence from Yemen." *Journal of Development Effectiveness* 9 (1): 1–14.

McKenzie, David, and Christopher Woodruff. 2021. "Training Entrepreneurs." *VoxDevLit* 1 (2). https://voxdev.org/lits/training-entrepreneurs.

Monreal-Pérez, Joaquín, and Valeska V. Geldres-Weiss. 2019. "A Configurational Approach to the Impact of Trade Fairs and Trade Missions on Firm Export Activity." *BRQ Business Research Quarterly* January. https://doi.org/10.1016/j.brq.2018.11.001.

Nedayvoda, Anastasia, Fannie Delavelle, Hoi Ying So, Lana Graf, and Louise Taupin. 2021. "Financing Deep Tech." EM Compass Special Note. International Finance Corporation, Washington, DC. http://hdl.handle.net/10986/36566.

OECD (Organisation for Economic Co-operation and Development). 2021. *The OECD DAC Blended Finance Guidance.* Paris: OECD Publishing. https://www.oecd-ilibrary.org/development/the-oecd-dac-blended-finance-guidance_ded656b4-en.

Ornelas, J. R. H., A. Pedraza, C. Ruiz-Ortega, and T. C. Silva. 2019. "Winners and Losers When Private Banks Distribute Government Loans: Evidence from Earmarked Credit in Brazil." Policy Research Working Paper 8952, World Bank Group, Washington, DC.

Peter, Caspar David, and Jochen Pierk. 2021. "Does Shark Tank Enhance Entrepreneurial Activities?" Available at SSRN. https://doi.org/10.2139/ssrn.3657391.

Piza, Caio, Tulio Antonio Cravo, Linnet Taylor, Lauro Gonzalez, Isabel Musse, Isabela Furtado, Ana C. Sierra, and Samer Abdelnour. 2016. "The Impact of Business Support Services for Small and Medium Enterprises on Firm Performance in Low- and Middle-Income Countries: A Systematic Review." *Campbell Systematic Reviews* 12 (1): 1–167.

Robinson, David T., and Angelino Viceisza. 2021. "Can the Media Spur Startup Activity? Evidence from the ABC Show Shark Tank." Unpublished working paper. http://gsf.aalto.fi/seminar_papers/shark_tank.pdf.

Viederyte, Rasa. 2016. "How Corporate Decisions Force Innovations: Factors and Choices to Act." *Procedia Economics and Finance* 39: 357–64. https://doi.org/10.1016/S2212-5671(16)30336-7.

World Bank. Forthcoming. "Advancing SMEs' Growth and Productivity towards Better Government Support in SME Access to Finance." World Bank, Washington, DC.

World Bank Group. 2021. "Strengthening World Bank SME-Support Interventions: Operational Guidance Document." World Bank, Washington, DC. https://documents.worldbank.org/en/publication/documents-reports/documentdetail/183521617692963003/strengthening-world-bank-sme-support-interventions-operational-guidance-document.

www.ingramcontent.com/pod-product-compliance
Lightning Source LLC
Chambersburg PA
CBHW041446210326
41599CB00004B/151